From the author of *The Hunters and the Hunted:*

Seeing David in the Stone

Find and Seize Great Opportunities
Using 12 Actions Mastered by
70 Highly Successful Leaders

James B. Swartz and Joseph E. Swartz

With contributions from Greg J. Swartz,
Julie K. Thorpe and Dr. John A. Swartz

Leading Books Press, Carmel, IN 2007

Published by Leading Books Press, Carmel, IN

For information about special discounts for bulk purchases go to leadingbookspress.com

Editing by Arlette Ballew
Cover design by Patrick Perry, August Associates
Cover management by Lisa Hoffert
Typesetting by Diane Collins
David photographs used with permission of Jon Sall
Drawings by Kathleen M. Swartz

Manufactured in the United States of America

Dardenn and Delyon Companies and their employees are fictitious. Any resemblance to companies or persons, living or dead is purely coincidental.

ISBN 0-9779456-5-0

Publishers Cataloging-in-Publication Data

Swartz, James B., Joseph E. Swartz
    Seeing David in the stone: find and seize great opportunities using 12 actions mastered by 70 highly successful leaders/ by James B. Swartz and Joseph E. Swartz
    Includes index and biographical references
        1. Success—case studies   2. Leadership   3. Innovation
4. Self-actualization

HD58.8.S92   2006

Dedication to:

James Bramsen,
for the opportunity to participate in his mission.

We are indebted: To the gifted writer **Debra Jobe** who made significant literary contributions to this book.

For priceless contributions to our work and our careers, **we are indebted to: Candice Somers,** who believed in us, and presented Jim with a major consulting assignment at McDonnel-Douglas
Lean pioneer and visionary, **Norman Bodek,** encouraged Jim to write.
Lean pioneer, **Ron Gill,** gave Jim the opportunity to study the Toyota production system in Japan in the late '70's.
Lee Sage gave Jim his 1st major consulting opportunity at Arthur Young in 1985.
Al Mataliano gave Jim his 2nd major consulting opportunity at Hughes in 1986.
Laura Louis and Jovita Vanover pioneered value stream mapping for us in 1986
John L. Mariotti taught us so much.
Ken Blanchard took an interest in the book.
Tom Endres and **Tom Stevens** gave Jim a great consulting opportunity at Cadillac in 1987.
Ernie Paskell, Frank Jaumot, and **Frank Stein** who nominated Jim for a fellowship to study with John Bardeen.
Paul Everett gave Jim a great consulting opportunity at Simpson Timber in 1990 and he made brilliant contributions to our thinking.
Tom Stevens, Parviz Daneshgari, and Ed Koerner gave us great consulting opportunities at GM Powertrain in 1991,
Don Fox gave Joe, Greg, and Jim the chance to make a difference.
Jennifer Marx gave us many important conceptual insights.
David Kasey, and Katie Enright inspired us.
Joe Benvenuto demonstrated a basic principle of leadership for us.
John Jones was our friend, our mentor, and our supporter.
Joe Strock taught us a lot.
Khristen Sohacki for her great advice at a critical point in our journey
Gary Brown for promoting our cause.
Ralph Olsen for an education in good leadership.

Jack Feller, General James McCarthy, Al Corrigan, Bill Waddell, Bruce Baggelly, Ory Fiume, Kathleen M. Swartz, Will Danesi, Joe Fragala, Evie Milliken-Coss, Tom Antczak, Vic Bach, Larry Edgar, Marge Garcia, Mike Fojtik, Vickie Sabatino, Marty Hynes, Christy Hofherr, Dan Vidusek, Dave Kouwe, Bob Whittier, Greg and Bryan Vrablik, Joe Strock, Ted Butterfield, Wayne Simon, Roger Nielsen, John Vaca, Doug Cluts, Chris DeHut, John Franco, Sal Garcia, Dale Lorenz, Kathy Errichiello, Susan Jennings, Frank Bramsen, Frank Raimondi, Frank Proano, Dominic Pelletier, Joe Ruelas, Larry Edgar, Janie Hutchins, Jim Rossum, Jim Rossum, Kevin Kaiser, Bob Adams, Jerry Hagers, Jerry Ferraza, Dave Smith, the other Jim Swartz, Sheri Law, Keith Hammer, Sam Manfre, John Williams, Ashley Andrew, Jane Miles, Marcia Moses,

Lisa Hoffert, Jan and Terry Nathan, Tim McClung, Jack Mandru, John Mirante, Tom Terpening, Michelle Thenin, Sue Mitchel, Tom Nguyen, Ray Noceda, Ron Olson, Karl Pasker, Linus Roy, Sam Sasry, Yelana Savchenko, Rudi Schick, Karen McGinnis, Judy Semon, Jim Simon, Russ Opre, James Neumann, Marcia Moses, Cynthia and Al Wosar.

Julie Thorpe thanks: Ralph Thorpe, Earl Strong, Carol Nealley, Susan Dunlap, Mary Collins Frank, Steve Kling, Jack Mandru, Kay Swartz, Laura Louis, Jovita Vanover, Conna Tigges, Stella Elting, and all the working mothers in my life.

Greg thanks: Jeff Settano, John K. Solheim, John A. Solheim, Doug Hawken, Kevin Point, Andrew Wert, Scott Fredrick, Mike Matusek, Scott Pflueger, Joseph Bruno, Dwayne Overstreet, Dave Forrester

Joe thanks: Julie Swartz, John Feller, Chuck Dietzen, Terry Munson, Heather Woodward, Tom Pearson, Paul Strange, Keith Jewell, Bob Brody, Alice Toth, Scott Whitlock, Dwayne Butcher, Jason Toschlog, Jim Huntzinger, John LeBlanc, Nik Janek, Marty Luffy, Paul Mezacapa, Tony Hoyet, George A. Pender, Bob Jarrett, Carl Rothenbacher, Jeff Sponaugle, Josh Overton, Jeff Kimbell, Deanna Suskovich, Thomas Eppel, and Richard Plapp.

Jim thanks: Ed Koerner, Dr. John Jones, Jerry Desjarlais, Louise Francesconi, Phil Larsen, Jerry Ferraza, Bill Kohley, Dave Foley, Rudi Schick, Dwight Callaway, Bob Sargent, Lee Sage, Deon Fourie, Greg Wahl, John Grom, Larry Weinberg, Jim Cameron, Bob Cameron, Don Carr, Jim Hall, Roger Dye, Melissa Glassburn, and Oliver Miller.

Acknowledgements: Those who reviewed the book and generously gave us feedback, including: Greg Bobeczko who made many valuable suggestions, Sandy Lucas, Mike Gardner, C. William Hanke, M.D., Season Harper Fox, Marilee Alsip, Michelle Rock, Ralph Thorpe, Natalie Swartz, Michael Thunder, Jim Washburn, Mary Suzan Bicicchi, Debbie Grant, Carla Eley, April Fugle, Elvia Magnana, Joe Fragala, Jim Prange, Michael Neff, Connie Moore, Patty DeMeo, Mary Beth Kennedy, Mary Lou Kozak, Tim Miller, Gary Paulsen, Jamie Jodscheit, Brendan Thorpe, Tyler Tigges, Maria Willer, Karla Stouse, and Bob Epperson.

And we are grateful to Maria Smith and the staff at Thomson-Shore.

For their assistance in research, John and Jim thank:
Dr. Rebecca Barrett, and Dr. Sajit Zachariah, University of Akron, Dr. Stan Bennett, University of Maryland, Dr. Walter Bennett, Sam Houston State University, Dr. Robert H. Berdan, California State University, Long Beach, Dr. David J. Bullock, Portland State University,

Dr. Richard Coffey, University of Utah, Drs. Ted Creighton, and Alice Fisher, the Leadership and Counseling Dept. Sam Houston State University, Ken Crowe, Northeastern Ohio University, Dr. David W. Dalton, Kent State University Dr. Jim Dorward, Utah State University, Dr. Thomas Fuechtmann, Loyola University, Chicago, Dr. Tom Griggs, San Jose State University. Dr. David Gullatt, Louisiana Tech University, Dr. R. Stanton Hales, College of Wooster, Dr. Larry Hannah, Cal State University Sacramento, Dr. Carl Harris Brigham Young University, Dr. Kendall Hartley, University of Nevada at Las Vegas, Dr. Mark Horney University of Oregon, Dr. Christina Hunt, Miami University of Ohio Dr. Robert C. Kanoy, University of North Carolina at Chapel Hill

Dr. Charlotte Kennemer, Stephen F. Austin State University, Dr. David Malone, Duke University, Chris Mc Williams, University of Houston, John McKay, Gustavus Adolphus College, Bonnie Mitchell, Bowling Green University, Drs. Richard Neville, and Helen Lafferty, Villanova University, Dr. John Park, North Carolina State University, Dr. Lynn Pesson, Louisiana State University, Dr. Richard Petrick, State of Ohio, Dr. Richard Pomeroy, University of California Davis, Dr. Regina Royer, Salisbury State University, Dr. Richard Rubenfeld, Eastern Michigan University. Dr. John Sanford, Wright State University, Dr. Jeff Shuckra University of New Mexico, Dr. Greg Smith, Lewis and Clark College, Portland Oregon, Dr. Michael Sofranko, Houston Community College, Dr. Al Strickland, Idaho State University, Dr. Sylvia M. Twomey Oregon State University, Dr. Robert Wagner, Ohio State University. Dr. Dante Zarlenga, USDA. Judy Williams @Ashland University.

M. J. Albacete, Canton Museum of Art, Ellen Banks, Youngstown State University Library, Rosanna O'Neil, Youngstown University. Judy Williams, Ashland University. Paul Culp, Sam Houston State University Library, Carolyn Dunlevy, ABC Washington, Carl Fisher, IBM, Barbara Hall, Hagley Museum and Library, Nancy Horlacher, Dayton and Montgomery County Public Library, Tim Johnson, Wilson Library, University of Minnesota, Thomas Keaveny, Hewlett Packard, Judi Keehnen, National Aviation Hall of Fame, Sue Hanson and Carmen Rodriguez, Case Western Reserve University Library, Jack Peet, Virginia Restoration Project, John Ring, Financial Services, Janet Stuckey, Special Collections, Miami university of Ohio, Michael Timko, Rockwell Industries, Gary Wakeford, CEO, SynchroMedical.

Diana Cornleisse, Wright Patterson Air-Force Base, Dr. Kenneth Gordon, Fellow of American Academy, Philadelphia, Jan Half, CA Technology Assistance Project, Cathy Nelson Columbus Public Schools, Candy Schneider, Clark County School District, Ted Perry, San Juan Unified School District, J. Judy Hennessey, Oakwood City Schools, Dayton, Ohio, Diane Talericho, Canton, Ohio Public Schools. Joanna Cole Whitley, Anderson County Schools, Tennessee.

Table of Contents

The Timeless Questions

*You cannot stay on the summit forever; you have to come down
again . . . so why bother in the first place?*

*Just this: what is above knows what is below, but what is
below does not know what is above. One climbs, one sees. One
descends, one sees no longer, but one has seen.*

Rene Daumel

For the last twenty years, we have searched for answers to three timeless
questions:

- How did some people find and seize the great opportunities of
  their times?
- What can we learn from them to help us find and seize great
  opportunities?
- How did great leaders help others (and organizations) to find
  and seize great opportunities?

In this search, we studied the lives, the works, the writings of, and
the past research on many successful people, including Michelangelo
Buonarroti, Winston Churchill, Marie Curie, Thomas Edison, Albert
Einstein, Dwight D. Eisenhower, Galileo Galilei, Bill Gates, Abraham
Lincoln, Fred Smith, Leonardo da Vinci, Sam Walton, Oprah Winfrey,
and Frank Lloyd Wright. We discovered that these and other great innovators and achievers all took the same actions to find and seize the
great opportunities of their times. It was these actions—rather than
heredity, traits, intelligence, environment, or work habits—that made
them more successful than others.

In recent years, we have been helping individuals and organizations to grow and prosper using these actions. We have proved that
anyone, at any age, can use these actions to become more successful.

Those who want to believe that success can be attributed mostly to
circumstances of birth, environment, or luck needn't read further. But
those who want to find and seize great opportunities can learn much
from studying the successes and failures of history's most successful
people and organizations.

We wrote this book to share with you the powerful actions that great innovators and achievers have discovered and used to find and seize great opportunities. We believe these actions are needed today more than ever. For example, in the past ten years, Asia's industrial might and innovative capabilities have risen rapidly. They can produce a lower-cost version of most products, a lower-cost alternative to many services, and they can do high-quality research and software development at a fraction of the cost of the same work done in the U.S., Canada, or Europe. In our competitive global economy, the ability to find and seize great opportunities has become a critical competence for survival for both individuals and corporations.

Great opportunities produce very high value for the time, effort, and resources required to find and seize them. By learning how to find and seize great opportunities, you will bring greatness to your own life and you will lead others to greatness.

How the Answers Are Presented

This book contains four parts. The first, "Mike Thom's Story," introduces the overall study and the way in which the lessons will be narrated. Part I describes how the successes and failures experienced by great innovators and achievers throughout history taught them how to position themselves for great opportunity. It describes the powerful learning processes they used and how they could imagine what seemed impossible to others. It also describes how they selected only those opportunities that gave them the greatest value for the least amounts of time, effort, and resources. Part II examines what they did to inspire other people to willingly give their time, effort, and resources to seize the opportunities and mobilize for action. Part III reveals how they focused their resources and the resources of others to rapidly and effectively seize the great opportunities.

We know how tiring it can be to read formal research, so we share our findings through the voice of Mike Thoms, president of the Dardenn Corporation. We hope that, as you follow Mike on his journey of discovery, you will learn the truths you need to find and seize your own great opportunities. As Michelangelo knew, there is a David in the stone; it is up to us to recognize it and make something of it.

James and Joseph Swartz
www.seeingdavidinthestone.com

Mike Thoms' Story

Earlier this year, I received a call from Marcus, the head of the research institute I had worked for as a young man. He told me that his research team had uncovered a powerful set of actions used by all the great innovators and achievers throughout history. He said that these actions explain how they found and seized the great opportunities of their times. He asked me to come to Italy to review the team's work. I agreed, and my life was changed forever by what I learned.

I took an overnight flight and arrived in Florence on a Tuesday morning. Marcus met me at the airport. From the moment I saw him, the three days in Italy were burned into my memory.

We exchanged the usual greetings of friends who hadn't seen each other in years. In front of the airport, a limousine driver loaded my bags into a car. "Santa Croce," Marcus said to the driver.

Once we were seated in the back of the limo, Marcus wasted no time getting to the point. He handed me a bound manuscript and said, "This manuscript is the result of our study of history's greatest finders and seizers of opportunity and what they learned from their successes and failures. It begins with the early failure of a great inventor."

Edison's Failure and Successes

"In eighteen sixty-eight, young Thomas Alva Edison won his first patent," Marcus began. "He was certain that the voting machine he had invented would make him and his investors rich. His patent described how wires would be connected from each congressman's seat to a central receiver, and how his machine would record votes immediately as each congressional member closed a "yes" or "no" switch at his desk. The young Edison told investors that the sale of his machines to legislatures would profit them over fifty thousand dollars—a half million in today's money.

"However, on his first sales call, his idea was immediately rejected by a Massachusetts legislator. Believing that the legislator was simply ignoring progress, Edison took the idea to Washington. On his first sales call to the U.S. Congress, a congressman listened a few minutes and then said, 'Young man, this is exactly what we don't want; the minority members want a chance to speak their opinions when they vote, and your invention would destroy their only opportunity to influence legislation.'

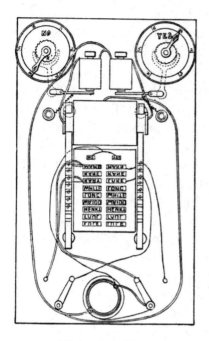

Voting Machine

"Edison was crushed. During his unhappy return to Boston, he licked his wounds. He decided to never again spend time on any invention not certain to have commercial demand. To all future ventures, he carried the lesson of the voting machine. Before he would commit his time, he would have to 'see' the entire system: the product itself, willing customers, price and costs that would ensure profit, and a practical distribution system for delivering the product to the marketplace.

"Nine years later, in an interview with a reporter,[1] Edison said that he was developing a light with no flame and no noxious fumes or smoke, that could be started with the turn of a screw and stopped at will. Unlike gas lighting, it would not blow out in the wind, and there would be no danger of explosion. He said that it would have flexible cords so it could be carried anywhere, that it could be operated upside down, and that the electricity that powered it could be used for heating and cooking as well.

"When John T. Sprague, a scientist, heard Edison's claims, he said, 'Neither Mr. Edison, nor anyone else, can override the laws of Nature. The talk about cooking food by heat derived from electricity is absurd.' Lord Kelvin, an eminent physicist, also scoffed at Edison's claims. Even when Edison had a working light, Professor Elihu Thomson said, 'Not only is the light too dim, but setting up a parallel circuit of many such lights and supplying direct current for them through conducting mains and branch wires would be too costly and impractical. It would need, in fact, all the copper in the world.'

"Can you see why Edison's critics were so wrong?" Marcus asked. "Can you see why he could find and seize an opportunity that the most educated scientists of the time couldn't see?"

"I'm not sure that I get the point you're making," I said.

"I'm saying that Edison's ability to find and seize opportunity can be traced to the failure of his first major invention, the voting machine. He knew that he had failed because of his lack of knowledge about politics and government. So, before he decided to invent an electric lamp, he studied gas-industry methods, seasonal curves of consumption, geographic distribution of gas usage, and the economics of gas lighting. An expert gas engineer said that by the time Edison invented the electric lamp, he knew more about the gas industry than anyone. Edison also studied the other electric-lighting pioneers of his time until he knew they were heading in the wrong direction with high-power arc lamps. He saw what was really needed: a low-power light for homes and businesses."

"I agree," I said. "Edison had monumental failures later in life when he ignored his own rule about making sure there were ready customers before he developed a product. For example, he mass-produced cement houses that very few people bought and he spent considerable effort and money on a talking doll that flopped."

"True," Marcus said. "His inventions in later life suggest that he disregarded some of the early lessons and, as we'll see later, he stuck to thinking that was obsolete for the times. He got wilder and less successful with age."

The way that Marcus spoke always amazed me—it was as if he were delivering a prepared speech. His sentences and paragraphs were always fully formed and articulate, just as they appeared in his published findings.

The driver stopped at Mario's café across from the church of Santa Croce. I carried the manuscript with me, and we went inside and ordered something to eat. When our order was ready, we seated ourselves in a corner. I said, "Most people say that hard work, perseverance, and the willingness to take a risk are the big factors in success."

Hard Work, Perseverance, and Risk Taking Are Not Enough

"There is no doubt that all who seized great opportunities were

Santa Croce

hard working and persevering," Marcus said. "But many people have worked hard, persevered, and taken risks, yet have never found and seized great opportunity. In his early career as a businessman, Edison worked hard, took risks, and persevered, but success eluded him. It was nine years later, after scientists said it couldn't be done, that Edison invented the first practical electric lamp. Galileo was a hard worker and took great risks to show evidence that the earth is not the center of the universe. But his antagonism toward those with different views alienated many powerful people of his time, and he spent the last years of his life under house arrest. Our research team wanted to know why so many other hardworking, risk-taking individuals and organizations failed. We wanted to know what some of them learned from failure so that they could find and seize the great opportunities of their times."

I nodded and smiled, saying, "A good example of risk taking and perseverance without success is Wile E. Coyote's pursuit of the Roadrunner." Marcus nearly cracked a smile.

I continued, "Peter Drucker,[2] who has been called 'the father of modern management,' says that none of the successful innovators and entrepreneurs he studied were inclined to be risk takers. He says they tried to define the risks they had to take and to minimize them as much as possible. He says they succeeded because they systematically analyzed, pinpointed, and exploited the sources of opportunity. In other words, they found great opportunities and then carefully managed the risks they needed to take to seize them."

"I agree with Drucker," Marcus said. "They succeeded only when they knew where the opportunity was and how to seize it. As I said, by the time Edison invented the electric lamp, he knew more than anyone on earth about the needs of the market and the technology of producing a practical lamp."

Heredity and Environment Are Not Enough

I said, "There also are those who say that great innovators and achievers were born with great minds and had great early environments. Examples often given are Mozart, whose father was a violinist and composer and trained him in music from birth, and Alexander the Great, who not only was the son of a king and a princess but who also was tutored by Aristotle."

Marcus replied, "There's no question that heredity and environment are important. But how do we explain why many brilliant people fail or never meet their potential? Why have some brilliant people created masterpieces, made important discoveries, or built

> *No one appreciates the agonizing effort Musashi has made. Now that his years of training have yielded spectacular results, everybody talks about his "God-given talent." That's how men who don't try very hard comfort themselves.*
>
> Yoshikawa Eiji[3]

great companies when many others haven't? What could da Vinci and Einstein have taught those who failed? Abraham Lincoln had an illiterate mother and a father who was a carpenter, yet he became one of the world's great leaders. Was it because he was more educated than his parents? Or did Abe follow a different path than they did?"

Being in the Right Place, with the Right People, at the Right Time Is Not Enough

I jumped in again. "There are those who say that the great achievers were in the right places, with the right people, at the right times."

Marcus shook his head. "Two-time Nobel Prize winner Marie Curie wasn't at the right place at the right time. She chose to be a scientist at a time when women were ignored in science. Instead, she made her own time and place, as we'll see later."

"I agree with you," I said. "There are people who say that Bill Gates was in the right place at the right time. But they don't know the whole story. His lucky break supposedly began twenty-five years ago when his friend, Paul Allen, walked by a newsstand in Harvard Square. A photo on the front cover of a magazine caught Paul's eye. The headline above the picture said, 'Breakthrough—World's First Minicomputer.' Paul grabbed a copy and ran across campus to tell Bill that the revolution had started without them. The next morning, Bill and Paul called Altair, the company that built the tiny computer, and claimed that they had a software program that would run on it. Then, in a two-week burst of creativity, they wrote a software program that did what they claimed."

"True," Marcus said. "Many leaders of major computer companies also saw that article and dismissed the tiny computer as a plaything.

Bill and Paul saw the potential. They knew that they had the software expertise and that, if they moved fast, they could seize the opportunity. Today, Microsoft—the company they built—is the largest personal-computer software company in the world, and both men have earned vast fortunes. So why didn't other software experts and leaders of large computer companies see the opportunity? They also were in the right place at the right time with the right people."

I said, "Marcus, I originally met you by being in the right place at the right time."

"No, Mike, you met me because you won a fellowship to study in my research institute. Your research was thorough and well documented, and you could back up your conclusions. Within a year, I put you in charge of the team studying innovative leadership because I saw that you had leadership capability."

"Were you upset when I left the institute to help Jesse Dardenn build his company?" I asked.

"No, I told Jesse all about you. I thought it was a great opportunity for you."

We Create Our Own Futures

"Mike, for centuries, people debated why some individuals and organizations became great," Marcus went on. "Theories that say it's because of heredity or early environment or being in the right place at the right time are 'life-lottery' theories of success. The life lottery is a comforting theory for those who have accomplished little. It's a hopeful theory for those who believe in luck. Because it says that most success factors are beyond an adult's control, it doesn't require much of us, nor does it inspire us to greatness. The great innovators and achievers didn't believe in a life lottery. They believed that we create our own futures and because they believed this, they searched for what they could do to find great opportunity.

"Leonardo da Vinci was born out of wedlock, which made him unable to be a member of a professional guild. Although he wanted to follow in his father's footsteps in the notary and business field, he wasn't allowed to. He chose art and science because illegitimate children were allowed in those fields. But he made the most of his choices and he created his own future."

"We can't control our heredity, and our early life environments usually are determined for us. But we can work hard, persevere, take reasonable risks, and try to be in the right place, with the right people, at the right time as our great examples did. We can do more than that. We can follow the same path to greatness as they did."

We sat quietly for a few minutes, finishing our meals, then Marcus said, "Mike, after you left the institute, we continued your research to identify how the people we studied had found and seized great opportunities. In your final report, you suggested that they all followed the same path. We now believe that we've discovered that path. In the next few days, I'll introduce you to many great innovators and achievers from whom we learned, beginning with a man who had an extraordinary ability to create masterpieces. First, we'll take a walk so that we can see the world as he saw it in the year fifteen hundred.

They All Followed the Same Path to Greatness

We left the café and walked west on Via dell' Anguillara. With the manuscript in his hand, Marcus walked rapidly, with an athletic stride. A few minutes later, we entered the Piazza San Firenze. Walls of dark stone rose four stories around us. Buzzing motor scooters swarmed at us like angry bees. Undistracted, he crossed the road to a massive, dark, fortress-like building with a bell tower. Like a duckling, I followed him up a flight of foot-worn stairs. At the top, he said, "We are entering the fortress Bargello. In Michelangelo's time, this housed the offices and torture dungeons of the dreaded secret police." He crossed a courtyard and ran up another flight of stairs, his footsteps echoing. A minute later, we stood before a sculpture of an effeminate boy, his foot on the severed head of Goliath.

"David, by Donatello," I said, reading the inscription.

We walked upstairs to another room to see Andrea del Verrocchio's bronze David. It was prince-like, with slender arms, a floral hat, and long curly hair. After looking at it for a minute, we left the room and walked down the stone stairs. "Have you ever heard of Verrocchio's or Donatello's or a hundred other Davids?" he asked.

"No, but I've heard of Michelangelo's David," I said.

David by Donatello

When we reached the street, Marcus pointed in the direction we were walking. "Five hundred years ago, Michelangelo Buonarroti walked these narrow streets, thinking of a great opportunity presented to him. The city of Florence had chosen him, instead of Leonardo da Vinci, to create a sculpture of David that would symbolize the city's three civic virtues: vigilance, fortitude, and anger at its enemies.

"Michelangelo concluded that the Davids created by past artists were weak and prince-like. He asked himself, 'Could they have protected Florence from her enemies?' Would you want the Davids you just saw protecting you?"

I smiled and shook my head.

Marcus said, "In a few hours, we'll see Michelangelo's David—a strong and powerful sculpture. It stands today as a supreme accomplishment in art. Michelangelo created such majestic works that

> *If anyone knew how hard and how long I have worked to beome what I am today, they would no longer think such great things about me.*[4]
> Michelangelo

many people called him 'divine' in his lifetime. This divine image of Michelangelo can lead us to believe that geniuses are born, not made. On the contrary, if his David was divinely inspired, he was given the inspiration only after he had spent thirteen dedicated years studying the works of the masters, working with master painters and sculptors, and learning the cultural values of his times.

"As I said, we found that all the great innovators and achievers, no matter what fields they pursued—business, medicine, law, finance, science, athletics, education, public service, the military, or the arts—followed the same path to greatness. This path consists of twelve powerful actions." He continued, "These actions enabled them to accomplish far more than others. We also found that successful organizations took these same actions. We'll focus first on the actions that individuals took."

The Twelve Actions Of The Great Innovators And Achievers

Marcus pointed to a drawing in his manuscript. "Here's a drawing that shows the actions the great ones took to find and seize great opportunity."

Marcus continued, "The four 'finding actions,' along with the four actions to mobilize support, are the first steps up the finding and seizing

Finding & Seizing Great Opportunities

Seize Great Opportunities
12. Develop other innovators and high achievers
11. Deliver rewards
10. Seize rapidly at high-leverage points
9. Use superior design and planning processes

Mobilize Support
8. Find common meaning with and negotiate with opposers
7. Sell the opportunity to those that are cautious
6. Co-create with those eager for opportunity
5. Find the highest meanings of others

Find Great Opportunities
4. Select only high-leverage opportunities
3. Learn to envision opportunities
2. Use powerful learning processes
1. Differentiate yourself for opportunity

mountain. Both sets of actions must be accomplished before you try to seize opportunities, as both Edison and Galileo discovered the hard way."

"Your use of the words 'great ones' bothers me," I said. "Some people don't relate well to lessons from giants like Edison and Gates."

"But what if the great ones all took the same actions to become great? What if even the most gifted people failed when they didn't take these actions? What if anyone could take the actions the great ones took?"

"That would convince me," I said.

"The great ones were convinced that, if life were a lottery, the winning numbers came to those who took these actions." Marcus was looking at me as if he were studying me. He knew I was hooked.

Find Great Opportunities

4. **Select only high-leverage opportunities**
3. **Learn to envision opportunities**
2. **Use powerful learning processes**
1. **Differentiate yourself for opportunity**

PART I

Four Actions to Find Great Opportunities

The secret of success in life is for a man to be ready for his time when it comes.[5]

Benjamin Disraeli

W e entered an open area and seated ourselves in an outdoor café just beyond the Campanile, a bell tower. As soon as we were settled, Marcus continued, "Let's begin our discussion of the first four actions:

1. Differentiate yourself for opportunity
2. Use powerful learning processes
3. Learn to envision opportunity
4. Select only high-leverage opportunities."

Campanille

Marcus explained, "An opportunity is a great opportunity if its value is far greater than the time, effort, and resources that are needed to seize it.

"Our next great innovator was a master in these first four actions, but especially in the first one: differentiate yourself for opportunity. We initially studied him, like Edison and Michelangelo, because of his legendary status as a genius. We wanted to understand how much of his success was because of inborn genius and how much was a result of the actions he took."

Differentiate Yourself for Opportunity

It is not enough to have a good mind. The main thing is to use it well.[6]

Rene Descartes

Differentiation And Success Factors

"There are many stories about Albert Einstein," Marcus began. "They say that, as a child, he was mentally slow; that he failed mathematics in his early school years; and that his teacher advised his father that he needn't concern himself with choosing a line of work for his son, because the boy wouldn't amount to anything. They say that Einstein was an outsider, an obscure clerk in a patent office who was ignored by his peers in science. Beyond the myth is a less dramatic story."

Young Einstein

"Einstein suffered from dyslexia and, up to age seven, he had difficulty speaking, having to repeat words to himself slowly. At age twenty, he obtained a degree in physics from the Swiss Polytechnic School, with a B average. Professors gave him poor evaluations, saying that he was rebellious and cut classes. With poor evaluations, he couldn't get a teaching post or a job in physics, so he took a job as a clerk in a patent office.

"For years, after working all day at the patent office, he returned to his drafty, one-room apartment in Zurich to spend his evenings studying the mysteries of time and motion. Then, in a flurry of writings, he proposed a new theory called 'The Special Theory of Relativity,' which

15

forever changed the face of physics." Marcus paused and looked at me inquisitively. "Was he simply a genius?"

"I would say so," I said.

"Our research team struggled with Einstein," he said. "Some people may say that lessons learned from geniuses don't apply to the rest of us. Then, one of our researchers asked, 'If Einstein had chosen to be a great patent reviewer, would we consider him a genius today?' We agreed that the answer was 'no,' because he had no passion for patent review; he was not exceptional at it, and since there was no opportunity in it to do something revolutionary, he had little chance of great rewards. His passion, talent, and potential rewards were in physics, and that's where he searched for opportunity."

Individual Success Factors

"The great ones knew where to search for opportunity. They searched on the basis of three factors: passion for the work, the potential rewards the work offered them, and what they were far better at than others. They chose to work where their abilities, their passions, and their potential rewards were all high. For example, young Edison chose to be a telegraph operator because he loved it, was good at it, and the telegraph was the Internet of his time."

Organizational Success Factors

"Where organizations choose to search also is very important," I said. "Noted researcher Jim Collins[7] found that corporations that had great performance over a fifteen-year period chose where they did business based on three factors: what they could be best at, what they had a passion for, and what drove their economic engines. These are the same success factors that great individual contributors used to choose their fields of work."

Finding Where to Search Late in Life

Marcus nodded. "Some people spend years searching for opportunity where the rewards will never be there for

Your High Opportunity Zone
is where you have a combination of high passion, strong expertise, and good reward potential.

them. But the great achievers never stop searching. Colonel Sanders is a good example. All his life, Sanders moved from sales job to sales job, living from paycheck to paycheck. At age sixty-five, he finally found where his opportunity was when he moved to Corbin, Kentucky, to run a gas station. To increase sales at the station, he started serving fried chicken made from his special recipe. Business boomed. Then a new interstate highway bypassed Corbin, and the business failed. Devastated, Sanders assessed his life. He decided that he knew how to fry chicken better than anyone else, he loved to cook, and he loved to sell. So he traveled the country calling on restaurants. He would cook each owner a batch of chicken, then sell a franchise. By age seventy-five, Sanders had six hundred franchisees. He never settled until he found a way to differentiate himself from the crowd and, when he did, he found great opportunity."

Changing The Ways In Which We Are Differentiated

Marcus added, "Collins found that great corporations also change late in life if they realize that they no longer can be best at what they do. He uses the example that, in nineteen sixty-four,[8] Abbott Laboratories knew that competitors like Merck had powerful laboratories that made them the best in the world at creating drugs. Although Abbott's core competence and principal source of revenue was drug production, its leaders knew that it couldn't be best in this field in the long run. So they searched for what Abbott could be best at. They decided to create products that make health care more cost effective, products that help a patient regain strength quickly after surgery, and diagnostics that improve a physician's ability to find the correct causes. Today, Abbot continues to be successful in the health care field."

"You're saying that great individuals and great organizations differentiated themselves in a similar way?" I asked.

"Yes," he said. "We also found that organizations that became great were led and managed by individuals who had learned to differentiate themselves personally. That's why we're beginning with how individuals used the actions.

"Great organizations like Abbott Laboratories are able to change the ways in which they are differentiated when one of their three success factors is no longer optimum. Often, however, organizations and individuals keep doing what they are best at and what they have a passion for doing in spite of overwhelming evidence that what they are doing isn't driving their economic engines anymore. For example, IBM went through an agonizing period in the early eighties, when the computing power of small, low-cost computers began to rise rapidly, and other companies were providing integrated solutions to customers. The leaders of IBM had a passion for building large, mainframe computers and they did it better than anyone else, so they continued to focus nearly all their resources on mainframes. They didn't transform IBM into an integrated-solutions provider until it suffered large financial losses.

"Some people and some organizations choose where they search for opportunity by weighing available alternatives—as if they were solving problems. The great achievers took a better approach. They analyzed areas of opportunity and asked themselves:
- What am I most passionate about?
- What can I do far better than others?
- What can bring me the highest rewards?

"Let us consider each factor in the light of a modern success story."

1. Differentiate yourself for opportunity
- What am I most passionate about?
- What can I do better than others?
- What will bring me the highest rewards I'm capable of?

What Am I Most Passionate About?

"In nineteen sixty-eight, two boys, Bill Gates and Paul Allen, were intrigued with a computer terminal that had been installed in their high school. They began to devote long hours learning to operate it. Within a year, twelve-year-old Bill wrote a small computer program to play tic-tac-toe. Although it took longer to play than it did with pencil and paper, Bill was fascinated with the program. Within a few years, the boys had learned enough to make money doing small programming jobs for local firms. They invested the money they made into more computer-terminal time. Both of them had so much passion for computer programming, they spent all their free time doing it."

What Can I Do Far Better Than Others?

"During those early days at the high school computer terminal, Bill realized he was not only good at computer programming, he could be far better at it than anyone else. Like Bill, most of the great innovators and achievers discovered from experience what they did well and what gave them uniqueness and a competitive advantage compared to others."

I interrupted. "There's some recent research by Buckingham and Coffman[9] that says that the most successful managers focus on what people do better than others and then place them in the organization where they'll perform best."

"Makes sense," Marcus said.

What Will Lead Me to the Highest Rewards?

"In nineteen seventy-two, Bill and Paul bought one of the early microprocessors and tried unsuccessfully to program it to run BASIC. So they programmed the microprocessor to measure traffic data. The traffic machine worked but was not a commercial success. Through these failures, they began to believe that they could make money in the computer business if they just found the right application. Then, as I mentioned before, in January of nineteen seventy-five, they discovered that Altair was advertising a small, four-hundred-dollar computer.

"They feared that the computer revolution had started without them. But they noticed that the advertised computer had rows of switches on its front plate that had to be programmed by hand, meaning that it didn't come with any useful programs. As I mentioned before, they immediately told Altair that they had a BASIC program that would run on its machine. Then they worked around the clock to prove they could actually do it. Bill wrote the BASIC[10] program while Paul found an ingenious way to test the program on a large mainframe computer.

"Then Paul flew to Altair's headquarters in Albuquerque. In the presence of the owner, he held his breath as he loaded the program. When the teletype printed the word 'ready,' he typed in 'print 2 + 2.'

Immediately the teletype printed the answer '4.' All those watching knew that they'd just witnessed the birth of a personal computer. Altair's owner was ready to make a deal. Bill and Paul were in on the ground floor.

"They chose where to search for opportunity based on what they could be rewarded for doing, what they had a passion to do, and what they could do better than anyone else. Paul quit his job at Honeywell, and Bill dropped out of Harvard. They named their new company Microsoft."

Life Purpose Is Woven into Each Differentiating Factor

"Purpose is a powerful driver of passion," Marcus said. People who find high purpose in their work also have high passion for the work. People who can do something far better than others often find high purpose in sharing their talents and expertise with others. When we are rewarded highly for what we do, we are able to support our families, we can contribute to the lives of others, and we can use our resources to influence important community and world events.

"The great scientist, Marie Curie, was driven early in life with the purpose of obtaining a Ph.D. at a time in Europe when no woman had ever been awarded a Ph.D. Knowing what she was up against, she differentiated herself by choosing physics, a field for which she had passion, in which she was far better than others, and where she thought she might be able to get a Ph.D. Later in life, when she had been highly rewarded, she made it her purpose to do what she could to cure cancer."

Marcus paused, summoned a waiter, and ordered espresso. I ordered cappuccino and a pastry.

He continued, "After determining where they had the best chances of finding opportunities, the great ones devoted a great percentage of their time to learning the most valuable knowledge and skills of the fields or markets in which they chose to find their opportunities. In doing that, they discovered some very powerful learning processes. In other words, after they decided where to search, their next action was to find what was best to learn and how to best learn it. Our next example was an exceptional learner. He knew how to identify important expertise and how to use it to create the largest corporation on earth."

Use Powerful Learning Processes

*Those who want to experiment without possessing some
knowledge are like navigators who set sail without a rudder or a
compass and who are never sure where they are going.*[11]

Leonardo da Vinci

"*I*t was nineteen forty-five, World War II was over, and the U.S. was adjusting to the end of rationing," Marcus began. "Beef and butter could again be purchased in any quantities. The wartime rules allowing the manufacture of only black, white, and brown clothing were lifted, and clothes could now be purchased in many colors.

"On Front Street, in the heart of the cotton town of Newport, Arkansas, John Dunham owned a store with annual sales of one hundred fifty thousand dollars. The Ben Franklin store across the street was a loser, with annual sales of seventy thousand dollars and a high lease of five percent of sales. When he learned that a returning soldier had bought the store, he felt pity for him. So when John found the man roaming in his store, checking on his prices and displays, John was glad to answer his seemingly endless questions.

"Initially, John was amused by the young man's wild promotions: a popcorn machine out on the sidewalk, a Ding-Dong ice cream machine, and a sale of ladies panties at four for a dollar. But John's amusement was short lived. In a few years, the soldier's sales exceeded his. To counter the threat, John decided to lease the property next to his store and expand. But he made a mistake by discussing his plan with friends. When he drove to Hot Springs to sign the lease, he got the shock of his life. The lease had already been signed by the friendly returned soldier, Sam Walton.

Lifelong Learning
"Throughout his life, Sam studied the expertise of the competition. Once, when he heard that a retail store in Minnesota had placed all its

checkout registers at the front of the store instead of in each department, he traveled over five hundred miles on a bus to learn how it worked. When he introduced the practice in his stores, he found that it not only saved shopper's time; sales actually increased. His thirst for knowledge never ceased. Years later, after he had already built his sprawling empire, he traveled to South Africa to learn the expertise of a small retailer who was doing exceptionally well. For twelve hours per day, as a guest of the small retailer, he visited stores, examined floor designs, checked inventories, questioned customers, and talked with vendors—taking notes all the while. He believed that anyone who was successful, even in a small way, had expertise worth learning. He also had the humility to ask others to teach him.

"In two thousand one, Wal-Mart became the largest corporation on earth, with over two hundred billion dollars in sales and over one million employees.

"To understand how the great ones learned faster and better than others, I'll be using the word 'expertise' a lot. By expertise I mean extensive knowledge and ability gained through study and experience. Sam and other great achievers found the answer to three important questions about expertise:

- Why is expertise so valuable?
- Which expertise is the most valuable?
- What are the most powerful ways to learn expertise?"

Why Is Expertise So Valuable?

Marcus continued, "Popular books don't stress the importance of expertise in achieving success, but researchers agree that it's the most critical factor. Pablo Picasso referred to its value in describing an incident that

2. Use powerful learning processes
- Why is expertise so valuable?
- Which expertise is the most valuable?
- What are the most powerful ways to learn expertise?

took place on a sidewalk in Paris. He was sketching when a woman spotted him and asked to be portrayed. He agreed. In minutes, she was depicted in an original Picasso. When the woman asked what she owed him, Picasso said five thousand francs. Surprised, she protested that it had only taken three minutes. 'No,' Picasso told her. 'It took me all my life.'[12]

"Frederick Douglas also knew the value of expertise. In eighteen twenty-seven, as an American slave, he was sent to live with a white plantation family. For the first time in his life, he walked on carpets instead of dirt floors and he had shoes and a hat to keep him warm. He no longer shared corn mush with other children from a trough on the floor.

> *Knowledge is power.*
> Francis Bacon

"He was intrigued that the family members read books and he begged the lady of the house to teach him how to read. One day, a few weeks into the lessons, as she was praising the boy's progress, her husband flew into a rage, telling her that she was breaking the law; if she taught the boy to read, he'd be unfit to be a slave. He said that the boy should know only the will of his master.[13]

Frederick Douglas

"Overhearing this, Douglas was hurt. But he also was impressed. If reading was that valuable, he wanted to read. From that day on, he hoarded scraps of printed paper as if they were gold. While he worked long hours in a factory, he studied newspapers that he nailed up at reading height. At age thirteen, he purchased his first book,[14] *The Columbian Orator,* with money he earned by shining shoes. He believed that learning was an opportunity rather than a chore."

I added, "Like freedom, it's an opportunity we don't appreciate when we have it."

"Yes," Marcus agreed. "Douglas escaped from slavery and, at great risk, he toured the U.S., speaking for emancipation. He wrote a best-selling book about life as a slave and founded the first black-owned newspaper. During the civil war, President Lincoln sought his counsel on the

Expertise: Extensive knowledge and ability gained through study and experience:

Emancipation Proclamation. In eighteen seventy-one, he promoted the passage of constitutional amendments banning slavery, making citizens of all people born in the United States, and outlawing racial discrimination in voting. Expertise set Douglas free, and he set others free."

Marcus opened the manuscript on the table and pointed to a box in the text. "I included some opinions of major researchers on the importance of expertise," he said.

The Importance of Expertise

Dr. Teresa Amabile,[15] a leading creativity researcher, says, "Being creative is like making a stew. The essential ingredient, like the vegetables and meat in the stew, is expertise in a specific area. No one is going to do anything creative in nuclear physics unless that person knows something, and probably a great deal, about nuclear physics."

Howard Gardner,[16] the creativity guru from Harvard, analyzed the talents, personalities, and work habits of Albert Einstein, Sigmund Freud, Mohandas Gandhi, Martha Graham, T.S. Eliot, Igor Stravinski, and Pablo Picasso. In all cases, their creative breakthroughs took place after ten years of study and the acquiring of experience—time in which they devoted almost their whole beings to their chosen fields.

The prolific inventor, Jacob Rabinow, said, "If you're a musician you should know a lot about music . . . if you were born on a deserted island and never heard music, you're not likely to be a Beethoven . . . you may imitate birds but you're not going to write the Fifth Symphony."[17]

Our waiter interrupted to serve our drinks and my pastry. Marcus paused to sip his espresso.

Expertise Versus Heredity and Circumstance

He continued, "Some people downplay the importance of expertise. They say that leaders are born to lead or have certain personality traits that make them good leaders. Some say that leaders become great because they're in great organizations or because of the situations in which they are leading. They use Winston Churchill as an example of a leader who became great because World War II occurred during his term of leadership.

"The fact is that Churchill had been an influential military and government leader for thirty-five years prior to World War II. He became a national hero in eighteen ninety-nine for his daring leadership and his escape from imprisonment in South Africa. He was elected to Parliament for forty years in a row, beginning in nineteen twenty-four. He was an expert on history and saw the future as few have. He warned the world about Hitler many years before Hitler's evil was apparent to others. In the late nineteen thirties, Churchill vigorously and publicly opposed those who appeased Hitler by allowing him to take portions of Poland and Czechoslovakia. As war broke out in Europe, Churchill was asked to serve as leader of the British Admiralty. He devoted himself to building up the navy and developing anti-submarine warfare. When Chamberlain resigned, King George asked Churchill to become Prime Minister and to lead the British war effort. By this time, Churchill was an expert in government, the military and leadership. His expertise proved crucial to winning the war.

"After the war, in early nineteen forty-six, years before others saw the path the Soviet Union would take, Churchill coined the expression 'Iron Curtain' to warn the world that the Soviet Union was taking over Eastern European countries."

I asked, "These 'great ones' you're talking about are all giants. How do you know that the same actions are important to people who aren't giants but who make smaller, but still valuable, contributions? Do these actions really apply to everyone?"

"We relied on your earlier research on lesser-known achievers to answer that," he said. "We studied only those who had sustained success for at least ten years. We were searching for actions that will stand the test of time—that will be valid one hundred years from now."

Expertise and Opportunity

I nodded. "I have someone who qualifies," I said, "Vito Pascucci. In high school, Vito learned to repair musical instruments. When he went into the army during World War II, the great bandleader, Glenn Miller, heard of his repair skills and had Vito assigned to his band. After Paris was liberated toward the end of the war, Vito's job was to drive a truck with all the band's instruments to Paris. Miller flew. Vito and Miller planned to visit musical-instrument manufacturers while they were in Paris, so they could open music stores across the U.S. after the war. It was the dream of a lifetime for Vito.

"When he reached Paris, Vito was devastated by the news that Glenn Miller's plane was missing—lost at sea. The dream was over.

"When the shock wore off, Vito visited instrument companies himself. During one visit to a factory, his life took another turn. His tour guide told him that the company wanted to sell instruments in the U.S., but instruments lost their performance during sea shipment. Vito told him to give the wooden parts time to stabilize in the new atmosphere in the U.S. If they were then reassembled, adjusted, and tested, he was sure they could be restored to factory specifications. Impressed, his guide invited him home for dinner. The guide turned out to be the manufacturer's son, Leon Leblanc.

"After the war, Vito set up a Leblanc office in the U.S. By day, he restored instruments shipped from France to factory condition. At night, he wrote to retailers and distributors. Sales grew so fast, the French factory couldn't keep up. So it had Vito build a plant in the United States. Years later, Vito bought a controlling interest in the entire company. Leblanc has won every award for musical instruments and, today, is a world symbol of performance and quality."

"Vito is a good example," Marcus said. "It shows the importance of expertise in finding and seizing opportunities. Vito found the opportunity with Glen Miller because he was an expert in his work. Misfortune took that opportunity away. But the Leblancs offered Vito another great opportunity because Vito had the expertise. The great ones like Vito considered expertise so important, they devoted themselves to becoming 'expert-insiders.' Let me explain."

Becoming an Expert-Insider

Marcus leaned toward me. "Many people say that insiders are too biased to create new ideas; that new ideas always come from outsiders. We have found that this isn't true. They called Einstein an outsider because he didn't work with any of the great physicists of his time before he developed his Special Theory of Relativity. However, Einstein graduated from Swiss Polytechnic and he was more of an expert in his field than any person alive when he made his breakthrough. Edison was considered an outsider because he finished only the fourth grade and wasn't part of the existing lighting market. But, as I said earlier, before Edison's team invented electric lighting, he and his team had extensively studied what other pioneers in electric lighting had done and they knew they could invent a light that would be far superior to anything that had been invented. In other words, they knew more than anyone else. Bill Gates was considered an outsider, but he and Paul Allen knew more about personal-computer software programs than anyone else in the world at the time. In other words, Einstein, Edison, and Gates were expert-insiders.

"A second type of insiders, power-insiders, have the power and control the resources in a field, but they seldom come up with the big innovations—according to the research that Burton Klein[18] did on twentieth-century innovations. Research done by Jewkes[19] also revealed that expert-insiders who were 'outside' their industries came up with almost all the big innovations in the eighteenth and nineteenth centuries.

"In other words," he said, "while less-successful people around them were waiting to win the life lottery, the great innovators knew that the chances of finding and seizing great opportunities are higher for those who have high expertise in their fields."

"I agree that expertise is very important," I said. "Years ago, when I was heading the innovative-leadership project for you, I saw how intensely the successful people learned about their work. But people don't want to hear about spending a lot of time learning. Many popular books tell us that power and creativity are within us, and we just have to find ways to release and harness them."

"Power and creativity are within us," he affirmed, "but we have to develop the expertise to tap into them."

I said, "Many people today are looking for drive-through success."

Marcus grimaced. "Certainly, Einstein, Gates, and Abbott Laboratories spent a great deal of time in preparation. But even small investments in preparation pay off. If Edison had spent a little time studying the market for an electric vote recorder, he wouldn't have wasted his time and other people's money on it. He learned the value of a small amount of preparation when he failed. From then on, he spent a lot of his time learning.

"The great ones spent a lot of time learning about their work and their markets but they also knew that the amount of expertise they needed to have was greater than they could ever learn with ordinary learning processes."

"It's hard to believe that they thought anything was beyond them," I said.

"We may think they were superhuman, but they knew they weren't," he said. They saw the obstacles and overcame them."

Overcoming the Obstacles to Gaining Expertise

"The available expertise of any field is large and growing rapidly," Marcus said. Tens of thousands of books and articles are published each year.[20] Yet we have the same twenty-four hours a day and no better minds than those who lived in Michelangelo's time. With ordinary approaches, we have no hope of becoming expert-insiders."

"But we live twice as long, on the average, and we have information systems and communication technology that they didn't have," I said.

"True, but the world is more complex and demanding. How much time do you spend expanding your expertise in the fields of business and executive leadership?" he asked.

"Not as much as I'd like," I replied.

He leaned toward me, his eyes gleaming. "To repeat, the great ones knew the importance of expertise to success and they knew that the amount of expertise in their fields was greater than they ever could learn. So they 'leveraged' their time, brainpower, and resources."

High-Leverage Focus

"The great ones focused on the expertise that was most valuable in their work or their markets. In other words, they always set themselves up to get the largest rewards for the time and resources they spent. Their thinking is based on the ancient principle of leverage. Mike, you've studied physics. How far back does the mechanical principle of leverage go?"

"Way back," I replied. "The earliest humans discovered how to use mechanical leverage to go beyond their physical limitations. They found that a person easily could lift a one-ton weight with a well-designed lever. I think that Archimedes first put the principle

High-Leverage Focus: Focusing the smallest amount of time and resources to produce the maximum gain toward your goals

in writing in two hundred B.C. To make his point he said, 'Give me a lever and a place to stand and I will move the earth.'"

"In the same way," Marcus said, "the great ones discovered the mental equivalent of the mechanical lever. They looked for where they could focus the smallest amount of time and resources to produce the maximum gains toward their goals. This took them beyond the limits of the normal human mind and beyond the limits of their personal time and resources.

"Both Leonardo da Vinci and Thomas Jefferson used high-leverage thinking by seeking expertise from masters in their fields. Leonardo wrote memos to himself, such as:[21]

- 'Ask a maestro how mortars are positioned on bastions by day and by night.'
- 'Get the master of mathematics to show how to square a triangle.'
- 'Find a master of hydraulics and get him to show how to repair, and the costs of repair, of a lock, canal and mill.'

"In seventeen sixty-nine, Jefferson was elected to the Virginia Assembly. Although he was already a well-educated man, one of his first acts was to order and read fourteen books, written by the giants in the field, on the theory and practice of government."[22]

Which Expertise Is the Most Valuable?

"Sam Walton had the ability to identify the expertise that gave him the best chance of success, compared with the time and effort he had to spend acquiring it. After he had multiple stores, he decided that his company needed expertise in computers and that someone else could achieve that better than he could. He attended an IBM class on information technology, with the purpose of hiring a person from the class who could lead that effort, and he did.

"This is called high-leverage expertise and, fortunately, it's only a small part of all the expertise in an area of work."

"How does a person new to a field identify the high-leverage expertise?" I asked.

> **High-Leverage Expertise:**
> The knowledge, ability, and experience that provide the highest chance of finding opportunity, compared to the time spent learning

"Where would you find it for trout fishing?" Marcus countered.

"A trout-fishing guide," I said. "I hired one a few years ago on a vacation. He taught me enough in four hours that I caught two, large, brown trout."

"What did he teach you?"

"To hold a tiny net at the surface of the fast-moving water to find the most frequent insect, because the trout will always bite on the one that's most plentiful." I smiled. "I guess that makes them high-leverage thinkers."

"Yes," he agreed.

I continued. "Then the guide gave me an artificial fly that matched that insect and taught me to cast upstream of the fast-moving water and to let the fly drift naturally."

"That's high-leverage expertise," Marcus said. "When I asked masters which expertise was the highest leverage in their fields or markets, they said it was the fundamental concepts and principles; the significant patterns; and the best processes, tools, and technology of the field. Let's consider each type of expertise."

Fundamental Concepts and Principles

"Although the tools of carpenters have changed, the fundamental concepts and principles of carpentry are the same as they were for the ancient builders of ships and buildings. A thousand years ago, master carpenters knew how to design roof trusses that would support a roof for a thousand years without sagging."

"On the other hand, the key principles of medicine have changed greatly. Doctors no longer believe that draining the blood from a patient will eliminate a disease. One hundred fifty years ago, doctors didn't sterilize before an operation because they believed that tiny germs couldn't kill people."

"Edison always identified the fundamental concepts and principles he had to learn to invent his newest product and he either learned them himself or he hired an expertise-insider. For example, scientists of Edison's time said that light bulbs would never be used in the home because they used too much current and there was not enough copper in the world to carry the current to millions of homes. So Edison hired Francis Upton, a Princeton physicist, who knew the design principles needed to produce a low-current filament for a light bulb. Edison and

Upton came up with a design that used only one percent of the original current. The design concepts they developed are still used today to make incandescent light bulbs."

Significant Patterns

"The researcher Christopher Alexander[23] concludes that patterns are the sources of creative power in individuals who use them; without patterns, they can create nothing. He says that a man who has a great deal of experience building houses has a rich and complex set of patterns from which to work. If you take his patterns away, he can do only simple building tasks.

"Those who learn the patterns of stock prices or the pattern that a wide receiver runs on a football pass play see a rich world of relationships and designs that others cannot see. The Velcro fastener was inspired by the pattern that allows seed burrs to stick to trousers. The inventor of the pull-top tab for soda and beer cans was inspired by the way a banana peels. Leonardo da Vinci advised that we take the time each day to study the world around us for its patterns."

Best Processes, Tools, and Technologies

"A master carpenter also has a vast storehouse of processes for shaping wood, such as sawing, drilling, routing, and sanding. Once a carpenter visualizes what he wants to construct, he will select and use the best process he knows and the best tools he has for each step in the construction," Marcus said.

"Do you imagine that Dardenn would have survived if you hadn't adopted modern technologies in your manufacturing areas and computer-aided-design technologies in your product-development areas?"

"We'd be out of business by now," I said.

Creatively Combining Expertise to Create New Products

"Expertise is growing so fast, Marcus said, "that few people today can become expertise-insiders in more than one work area at a time. However, many major innovations are the result of creatively combining the expertise of many fields. So, to create a light bulb, Edison hired experts in glassblowing, vacuum technology, chemistry, physics, machining, magnetics, model making, and electricity. He managed this team of experts to creatively combine their expertise.

"To create computer-animated motion pictures, such as *Toy Story, A Bug's Life,* and *Monsters Inc.,* Pixar's founder, Ed Catmull,[24] brought together expert artists along with experts in computer programming and animation. Each person was cross-trained in the tools Pixar uses and in filmmaking, sculpting, drawing, painting, and improvisation."

Finding the Sources of High-Leverage Expertise

"The great masters sought other masters to identify which concepts, principles, patterns, processes, and tools were most valuable in their fields or markets. They read the writings of the masters, attended their lectures, and worked with them. They hired or collaborated with people who had great expertise."

"Some people say it's not what you know but whom you know," I said.

Marcus said, "Our research says the expression should read 'it's not only what you know but whom you influence.' Many who were in the right place at the right time didn't see an opportunity because they lacked expertise in the fields they were working in. Others knew the right people but lacked expertise in influencing others. You need both expertise in the work and expertise in human behavior. Edison had expertise in electromechanical invention and in marketing his inventions through the press. Sanders had expertise in frying chicken and in influencing people to buy franchises."

I asked Marcus, "How do you convince someone that education is important when they know that Bill Gates dropped out of Harvard to start Microsoft?"

"At age eleven," Marcus replied, "Gates began his preparation to become one of the most knowledgeable people on earth in personal-computing software. He invested thousands of hours in learning the expertise he would need. By the time he dropped out of Harvard, he was highly prepared. But keep in mind that attending universities, technical schools, and vocational schools and working with masters are great ways to rapidly gain high-leverage expertise."

He cocked his head. "Let's explore your current field to determine which expertise an individual should learn to find great opportunity in management."

The High-Leverage Expertise of Management

"Management is complex work," Marcus said, "and mastering its expertise is difficult. "He pulled the manuscript toward him, thumbed through it, and pointed to a particular page. "In the shaded box, I have what Peter Drucker[25] says is the high-leverage expertise of managing."

High-Leverage Expertise of Management

- *Make people capable of joint performance*
- *Make their strengths effective and their weaknesses irrelevant*
- *Enable the enterprise and each of its members to grow and develop as needs and opportunities change*
- *Build performance into the organization—think through, set, and exemplify objectives, values, and goals*

Peter Drucker[26]

He continued, "Most executive managers began as individual contributors and then learned the expertise of each of the roles they had as they rose to higher responsibilities; just as you did on your way to becoming president of the Dardenn Company. They practiced what they learned and analyzed their successes and failures."

"Marcus," I interjected, "are you suggesting that we focus on just one area of work? Some people say that when we focus too much, we become narrow thinkers. They say we should be generalists."

"It's valuable to have knowledge of many fields and markets but, to find great opportunity, you should be a master of at least one," he replied. "Edison and Walton had to learn many types of expertise to build great companies, but each of them had to master the expertise of at least one field or market area before they broke through to greatness. With Edison, it was electromechanical invention; with Walton, it was discount retailing."

What Are the Most Powerful Ways to Learn Expertise?

Marcus leaned forward. "Even when they focused on learning the high-leverage expertise of their fields or markets, the great ones knew that they were still limited by time and the limits of their minds. So they found four powerful learning processes that allowed them to make the most of their limits. The four powerful learning processes are:

- Devote quality time to learning
- Manage the thoughts that occupy your mind
- Use deep processing
- Learn in the pursuit of opportunity."

I smiled. "Could these learning processes turn me into an Einstein?"

He smiled back. "Mike," he said, "without them, even Einstein wouldn't have turned into an Einstein. He had a fine mind, but many fine minds never found greatness."

I was pleased to be with my best teacher again. He drank some espresso and then continued. "Let's begin with the first powerful learning process: devote quality time to learning."

Devote Quality Time to Learning.

"Our next great learner was a master of this process. In the nineteen seventy-two Olympics, after placing tenth in the Decathlon, Bruce Jenner was watching a Russian receive the gold medal. Although disappointed after years of preparation, he asked himself what it would take to stand at the top of that platform. He decided to take every second of every day for the next four years and do only what prepared him to win at the nineteen seventy-six Olympics.[27] From then on, he used every spare moment to prepare—even placing a hurdle near his kitchen table so that he could rehearse jumping hurdles in his mind as he ate his meals.

"At the nineteen seventy-six Olympics, Jenner won the gold medal by the largest margin in history and set a new world record. This is an example of the ultimate in mind focus, the ultimate in making the most of our limited time as humans."

"All the great ones were acutely aware of the limits of their time," Marcus said. "When billionaire Bill Gates was asked what he could want more of, he said, 'More time.'[28] To get beyond the limits of time, we must find ways to increase the time we devote to learning and we must focus our whole beings on learning—as Jenner did."

I asked, "Are you talking about time management?"

He moved his cup to the side and leaned forward again. "The great ones managed their time. But there are major differences between the time management of the great achievers and those who accomplished less. Bill Gates also said, 'My success in business has largely been the result of my ability to focus on long-term goals and ignore short-term distractions.'

"Peter Drucker says: 'Everything requires time. It is the only truly universal condition. All work takes place in time and uses up time. Yet most people take for granted this unique, irreplaceable, and necessary resource.'

"Fortunately, preparing to find most opportunities won't take the devotion of a Jenner or an Einstein," Marcus said. "However, it takes thousands of hours of study and experience to become a sought-after doctor, executive, chef, plumber, or teacher. The greater the opportunities we seek, the more time we must devote to preparation. Great opportunities seldom are found by the unprepared. Because the great ones realized the long-term benefits of preparation better than others and also knew that they had little time, they devoted quality time to learning. To devote quality time to learning, we need to place learning high on our list of priorities; increase the percentage of time devoted to learning; focus completely when learning; and apply what we learn, measure the results, and relearn.

Let's move on to the second powerful learning process."

Manage the Thoughts That Occupy Your Mind.

He shifted a little and continued, "The second powerful learning process is to manage the thoughts that occupy your mind. Our brains can store unlimited knowledge and combine it in unlimited ways. They can process millions of subconscious thoughts per second. So why does it take over five thousand hours of study and experience to become a master plumber or machinist, ten thousand hours of education and experience to become a valuable knowledge worker, and five thousand more hours for a career in law or medicine? If our brains are infinitely powerful, we need to understand why it takes so long."

I said, "I've heard that we use less than five percent of our brains; if we could learn to use the rest, we would greatly increase our ability to think and create."

"Mike, more than ninety percent of each brain directs billions of unconscious actions that take place in the daily routines of living." He picked up his espresso. "Picking up this cup of espresso, bringing it to my mouth, sipping, and returning the cup to its saucer require millions of small electrical and chemical reactions that are coordinated in the brain. Complex tasks, such as driving an automobile and hitting a golf ball, require the coordinated action of dozens of subsystems in the brain. Even the great achievers couldn't use those parts of their brains for thinking and creating. But ten percent of their brains was enough, because they knew how to use that ten percent well."

One Thought at a Time. "One reason it takes so long to become an expert is that a brain can process only one conscious thought at a time. This is apparent to me when I forget what I just read or heard because another thought has entered my consciousness. We think of multiple things by alternating attention among them. We must store each thought and return to it a short time later—as if we're pushing pause and play buttons on multiple mind recorders."

One Thought Per Second. "Another reason it takes so long to learn expertise is that a conscious mind can process only about one thought per second, while the subconscious is processing thousands of thoughts per second."

Subminds. "The last reason for the long time it takes to learn is that our brains have hundreds of 'subminds' operating below consciousness. When you overhear a conversation with the word 'horrible' in it, see an attractive person, or think of something worrisome that your boss said, your submind goes into action. Brain researchers say that our subminds act independently, outside our conscious minds, and each wants to be the center of our conscious attention."[29][30]

"That reminds me of a scene in a movie with Groucho Marx," I said, smiling.

"Groucho plays the leader of a small country that's close to war. In the scene, Groucho is about to meet the ambassador of the other country. He's confident that his peace offer will be accepted. But then Groucho begins talking to himself as he paces back and forth. 'What if he snubs me by not shaking my hand? How will that look to my people? Why that cheap, no-good swine; he won't get away with it.' By the time the ambassador arrives, Groucho is fuming. His first words to the ambassador are, 'So, you refuse to shake hands with me!' He slaps the ambassador and starts a war."

Marcus smiled politely. "Like the thought of Groucho that entered your mind, our subminds intrude like thieves in the night. They distract us and sap our productivity. They produce chemicals that excite and depress us. When they dominate our actions, we ignore preparation and decrease our chances of finding great opportunities in the future. We are attracted by the exciting parts of our worlds, so we don't spend time creating our futures."

Controlling Intrusions. "If someone wanted to get better control, how would he go about it?" I asked.

"Catch the non-invited intruders as they enter your brain," he answered.

I'd hate to be a thought that entered Marcus's mind without invitation, I thought.

"Once I realized the power of highly focused time," he said, "I tracked intrusions into my mind until I identified my top intrusion for a week. Then I caught and stopped it each time it intruded. I used the time I saved to further develop organizations I served. I did this until I could do it without thinking about it."

"Do you have an example of an intrusion you stopped?" I asked.

"Yes. Any fire or crime I'd hear or read about would grab my attention. I'd find out if the police caught someone, why he did it, what kind of person he was, and what happened at the trial. I'm now in control of my time."

I smiled. In my wildest imagination, I couldn't picture Marcus out of control. "Are you saying that you ignore world events?" I asked.

"No. But modern media is swirling about us, competing for our attention while the expertise of any single area or field or market is increasing rapidly. More than our grandparents, we must control what we allow into our minds.[32] The great ones could focus—choose to have only valuable thoughts in their minds."

Our Time Is Filled. "You make the actions seem like a big investment of time," I said. "How can someone follow these actions if the person already is busy with a job, a family, and other commitments?"

"The person must believe as the great ones did: that investment in learning brings large future benefits and increases opportunities. By using the preparation actions of the great ones, whatever time the person spends on learning moves him or her rapidly on the path to opportunity. Somehow, we must carve out more time each day and devote it to learning our fields or markets."

I asked, "What about activities that don't contribute anything and don't increase our expertise in our fields or markets, like watching baseball?"

He almost smiled again. "Recreation is good for the spirit. But a serious musician will spend a Sunday afternoon with a musical artist instead of attending a baseball game because he knows the value of preparation or he loves music first. To willingly devote the time to our fields or markets, we must choose work for which both learning and working are recreational. If you're in work that you have no passion for, you must either change what you do or learn to love it."

Use Deep Processing.

"The brain is also limited in its ability to store, combine, and recall memories," Marcus explained. "To get around these limitations, the early Greeks developed some memorization techniques that are now universally taught. The techniques were made popular because of a terrible accident that took place at a banquet in four seventy-one B.C. After reciting poetry to the assembled group, the poet Simonides was called outside to meet some men. While he was outside, the concrete roof of the banquet hall collapsed, crushing the guests within. When he was asked if he remembered any of the positions and names of the guests, Simonides reproduced the entire guest list and where each guest was seated. When he explained how he used a system of mental images based on the location of each guest around the table, his learning methods immediately became popular. Although the use of visual images for memorization is effective—to some degree—for almost everyone, some people remember better what they hear, what they touch, or what they feel emotionally. It is important to use memorization techniques that are best suited for you.

Deep Processing Versus Memory Recall. "Although what Simonides did was remarkable, he was not being innovative, he was recalling images and facts. The ability to recall memories was not what enabled Simonides to write epic poems. Rather, it was his ability to store memories so that they could be creatively retrieved later. It is important to understand the difference between recalling something and creatively retrieving it. Let me give you an example of creative retrieval."

"In nineteen thirty-five, Edgar Kaufman asked Frank Lloyd Wright to design a small, summer home for him. But after Wright visited the site and had it surveyed, he did nothing. One day, Kaufman called him and said he was forty miles away and would like to see the design. 'Come on Edgar,' Wright said. 'We're ready.'

"Overhearing Wright's conversation, two of his primary draftsmen couldn't believe what he had promised. He had not drawn a single line. One draftsman, Edgar Tafel, detailed the scene that followed in his book about Wright:[31]

> Wright hung up the phone, walked to the drafting room and started to draw, talking in a calm voice. 'They will have tea on the balcony . . . they'll cross the bridge to walk into the woods,' Wright said. Pencils were used up as fast as we could sharpen them. He erased, overdrew, modified, flipping sheets back and forth. Then he titled it across the bottom: Fallingwater.

Two hours later, when Kaufmann arrived, Wright greeted him and showed him the front elevation. 'We've been waiting for you,' Wright said.

They went to lunch, and we drew up the other two elevations. When they came back, Wright showed Kaufmann the added elevations.

"Wright's Fallingwater made the front cover of *Time* magazine in January of nineteen thirty eight. The house is built on top of a waterfall that cascades through the lower level. Wright and his team were able to produce an award-winning design in a few hours because they had vast stores of expertise in their memories that had been developed over decades and which they could creatively retrieve. The key lesson here is that they didn't simply recall the memories they had stored; they retrieved new creative combinations of these memories—memories they had stored using a powerful learning tool: deep processing."

Storing Memories Using Deep Processing. "Research has shown[34] that one's ability to creatively retrieve memories is affected primarily by how one first puts something into memory. All the great ones used deep processing to store expertise so that they could creatively retrieve it later. They processed information deeper in their brains than less successful people did.[32] To deep process memories the way they did, you need to:

- Relate and compare what you're learning to the expertise you already have.
- Ask yourself what is similar, what is different, what is new, what agrees with what you already know, and what does not.
- Go beyond the superficial and ask, 'What is the special meaning of this expertise to me, to others, and to society?'
- Ask why you are better off knowing the expertise and what you can do with it.
- Question the expertise, think of its opposite, debate it with others, teach it, and review it several times in the coming days.
- Use your sight, your hearing, and your physical body to learn, but especially use the one that allows you to learn the best.

- Create images of the expertise in your mind combined with what you already know. Sketch the images or write descriptions of them.
- Learn with passion.

Creating Below the Conscious Level. "When we deep process expertise into memory, all the memories stored earlier are enriched, because the new memories interact with the old ones, and accumulated expertise grows like ivy. So when we retrieve a deeply processed memory, we can get new, creative, valuable patterns without consciously recalling the individual memories that are combined. The subconscious mind is not bound by conscious rules, so it can make creative combinations of stored expertise that the conscious mind won't allow."

"When Simonides recalled the people at the banquet, he brought individual memories to consciousness. However, when Simonides wrote great poems and when Wright designed Fallingwater, they creatively combined deeply processed memories in their subconscious minds. Then they brought the new creative combinations to the conscious level. In essence, the great ones were innovative primarily because they had great stores of deeply processed expertise that could be creatively combined in their subconscious minds."

Marcus paused and looked at his watch. "As we will see in about an hour, they also had special ways to coax their brains to combine their deeply processed expertise in new and wonderful ways."

Learn in the Pursuit of Opportunity.

"The fourth powerful learning process the great ones used was learning in the pursuit of opportunity. Researcher Edgar Dale[36] found that, two weeks after reading, hearing, or seeing something, we remember only ten percent of it. However, if we discuss it with others, the level of retention is increased to twenty to forty percent. Dale says that, when expertise has high meaning to us, when we have a purpose in learning it, and when we learn it directly through experience, we may remember as much as sixty percent of it two weeks later."

"Bill Gates said, 'There are people who can recall detailed information they have only scanned and never really thought about. I'm not one of them. I have a good memory, though, for information that I've been deeply involved with or cared about.'

"It has been consistently found that we learn the best and fastest when we are pursuing opportunities."

I said, "The opportunity-finding and seizing workshops you did with us at Dardenn were based on that principle. Immediately after you taught us the concepts and principles, we used them to find and seize cost reduction opportunity."

"Yes," he agreed. "Pursuing opportunities is the best way to learn, because we learn with a purpose; we deep-process what we learn; we are directly engaged in an innovative process; we challenge our strengths, which increases them; we reinforce what we learn through successes and failures; and we are passionate about what we are learning.[33] This is another reason that the great ones, like Einstein and Wright, learned faster and better than others. They were always preparing for, finding, and seizing opportunities. They were in constant pursuit of opportunity."

In summary, deep processing and learning in the pursuit of opportunity are the two most powerful learning processes of the great innovators and achievers."

Secret Strategies?

I said, "Twenty years ago, when our research team was investigating what made people great, we suspected that the great ones had secret strategies."

"The twelve actions they took could be considered secrets," Marcus said, "not because the great ones kept them secret but because only a few recognized their importance. Even when we began to teach adults how to apply these actions in their lives and organizations, many were skeptical. Since then, we have followed their careers and the success of their organizations. We have found that those who used these actions found and seized greater opportunities than those who didn't."

"Once we master these powerful learning processes, we can rapidly learn the expertise of the fields of work or markets we have chosen. Or we can use them to change jobs or start new businesses. Either way, we would identify which knowledge and skills are the most important; then we would devote quality time to learning and practicing them. We'd deep process what we learn, relating and creatively combining it with the knowledge and skills we already have. Then we would be ready to search for opportunity."

Summary

"To summarize so far: First, the great ones chose to search for opportunity where they had the best chance of finding great opportunity. Second, they became expertise-insiders by using powerful learning processes to learn the high-leverage expertise of their work." Marcus looked at his watch again. "Let's take a break before we talk about the third action."

Reality Intrudes

It turned out that learning about the actions of the great achievers changed my life. While I was in Italy, Dardenn's CEO, Ron Dardenn, took the opportunity to make some changes that caused me to bring many of these actions into play in order to survive professionally and to keep the company from disaster. That story started as soon as Marcus left the table and I checked my cell phone.

The first voice message was a warning of things to come. It was from Paul, the engineering director at Dardenn. He said Ron's brother, Larry, had come to him with an idea to save money by eliminating the over-pressure vent on the N-series products. When Paul told him that the vent was a safety feature, Larry said there was a one-in-a-million chance of failure and told Paul to do it. I checked the time back home, then I immediately called Ron's office.

"Hey, how's it going over there?" Ron asked in his best-buddy voice.

"What's this I hear about Larry wanting to eliminate the vent on the N-series?"

He cleared his throat. "I asked him to help out in manufacturing and engineering until you got back."

"But he doesn't have any expertise in manufacturing or engineering," I said.

"Hey, he's already found some good ideas for cost savings."

"Ron, the vent is a safety feature!" I protested. "Are you willing to risk lives to save a few pennies per unit?"

In a patronizing voice, Ron replied, "Keep an open mind. I'm due in a meeting. We'll talk later."

"Don't . . ." the phone went dead ". . . remove the vent," I said, for my own benefit.

I left a message on both Ron's and Larry's phones, warning them that they had to get permission from the customer, Delyon, before eliminating the vent.

Larry's decision to eliminate the vent pounded home the fact that, without expertise, we are not prepared to find great opportunities. When Marcus returned, he asked me if something was wrong. I told him that I had a problem but I could handle it.

"I'm sure you can," he said. He sat down. "We'll continue with the third action of the great ones: they learned to envision opportunity. At the beginning of the twentieth century, our next master envisioned a great opportunity. After her discoveries, scientists had a new view of the atom. I'll begin her story on the most frustrating day of her life, at the end of four years of intensive research and back-breaking labor."

ACTION 3.

Learn to Envision Opportunities

"No use trying," Alice said: "one can't believe impossible things."
"I daresay you haven't had much practice," said the Queen.
"When I was your age, I always did it for half-an-hour a day.
Why, sometimes I've believed as many as six impossible things
before breakfast."

Lewis Carroll[37]

"In eighteen ninety-five, Marie Curie obtained her undergraduate degree in physics from the University of Paris. As a woman at that time, she would not be considered for a doctoral degree, even though she was at the top of her class. However, she knew that if she made a breakthrough scientific discovery, she might have a chance."

Marie Curie

"X-Rays, a form of invisible light, had just been discovered by Roentgen. Using her scientific expertise, she predicted that the element thorium might emit invisible light. She bought large quantities of pitchblende, a naturally occurring ore that contained small amounts of thorium. She then chemically separated thorium from the ore and found that it did emit an invisible light. Then she made a crucial observation. After the thorium was removed, the remaining ore emitted more invisible rays per pound. Further separating the ore, she discovered a new element that she named polonium. Then there was a further surprise: the ore remaining after the extraction of polonium was thousands of times more radioactive than anything she had seen. She named it radium. To prove that it was a new element, she had to separate it from the ore."

"For four years, she crushed and chemically separated two tons of ore. As each compound was removed, the remaining material increased in radioactivity. Her husband, Pierre, became so excited by her findings that he abandoned the work he was pursuing and joined in her research. Then, one fateful day, after hundreds of separations, only a few ounces remained. She finished her last separation and waited anxiously as the chemicals worked.

"When the reaction finished, as she looked for the remains in the bottom of the reactor, she found nothing. The final separation apparently had eliminated the entire compound. She was devastated. At home that night, she wrestled with thoughts of what could have gone wrong. Maybe her detractors were right. They said she was looking for something that didn't exist. She couldn't sleep. If her theory that radiation came from the center of the atom was correct, it couldn't have been destroyed chemically. In the night, she returned to the lab.

"When she opened the laboratory door, it appeared as if a light had been left on. She walked quickly toward the glow. It was coming from the glass dish that held the remains of her last separation. The residue, invisible in the daylight, glowed intensely. She weighed it. It had no detectable weight but it was highly radioactive. She was jubilant. She had extracted enough pure radium to prove that it was a new element."

"In nineteen two, a doctoral examining board said that her findings were the most significant ever presented in a doctoral thesis and awarded her the first doctoral degree ever presented to a woman in Europe. Later that year, she became the first woman to win the Nobel Prize in Physics, for her discovery of radium. A few years later, she was awarded a Nobel Prize in Chemistry—becoming the first person to win a Nobel Prize in two different categories. As you know, the invisible rays from radium were later used for x-ray imaging and for treating cancer."

"To understand why people like Marie Curie see opportunities that others don't see, we have to answer three questions:
- What are the most creative behaviors?
- How can we see into the future?
- How can we visualize great opportunities?

"Our research discovered answers to each question."

What Are The Most Creative Behaviors?

"In his book, *Creating Minds,* Howard Gardner[38] defines a creative person as one who regularly solves problems, develops products, or defines new questions in a way that is initially considered novel but ultimately becomes accepted. Curie had all the valuable creative attitudes and behaviors of the great opportunity finders. These are:

- Put a high priority on creating and a low priority on consuming
- Search for original opportunities to create
- Learn expertise with healthy skepticism
- Challenge assumptions and rules
- Create a life that is a creative journey to the very end
- Create like a child, persevere like a soldier
- Leverage risk with expertise

"I will discuss each of these in order," Marcus said.

A waiter approached our table. Marcus waived him away, then turned his attention back to me. "The most common behavior of a person with a creative mind is based on his or her priorities."

Put a High Priority on Creating and a Low Priority on Consuming

"Curie was not only focused and hard working, she prioritized her use of time so that she spent most of it creating. An activity is creative if its end goal is a seized opportunity—such as creating or improving a product, service, system, or organization. For example, those who watch a football game are consuming. The creators are the coaches, owners, players, halftime producers, television producers, directors, cameramen, ad men, and the

3. Learn to envision opportunities
- What are the most creative behaviors?
- How can we see into the future?
- How can we visualize great opportunities?

architects and contractors who built the stadium. Creative people have more passion for creating than for consuming."

Search for Original Opportunities to Create

"Early in his career, before he sculpted David, Michelangelo applied for work at a commercial studio. In the book, *The Agony and the Ecstasy*, Irving Stone dramatizes the differences between Michelangelo's creative attitude and the attitude of the owner of the commercial studio.[36] The owner tells Michelangelo that his deliveries are never late because he knows 'within a matter of minutes how long each panel of fruit or spray of leaves will take to carve.'

"Michelangelo asks what happens if a sculptor thinks of 'something new . . . an idea not carved before?' The owner replies, 'Sculpture is not an inventing art, it is reproductive. If I tried to make up designs, this studio would be in chaos. We carve here what others have carved before us.' Michelangelo again asks him what would happen if a sculptor wanted to 'achieve something fresh and different.' The owner says, 'That is your youth speaking, my boy. A few months under my tutelage and you would lose such foolish notions.'"

"Of course, Michelangelo didn't take the job," Marcus said. "He was searching for an opportunity to do original, creative work."

Learn Expertise with Healthy Skepticism

Marcus continued, "Each year, before nineteen fifty-two, fifty thousand people were paralyzed for life with polio—the same number as were killed in automobile accidents.[37] It was believed at the time that a person had to experience a live virus to be immune. But Jonas Salk was skeptical of that theory. So he deactivated a live virus with ultraviolet light and injected it into humans. It worked, and a vaccine was developed that decreased the cases of paralytic polio to less than ten per year. Salk received the Presidential Medal of Freedom for his achievement.

"According to studies,[38] there's a difference in the way that creative people like Salk learn. Those without a creative attitude absorb knowledge without question, but those like Salk digest knowledge with a questioning attitude. One of Salk's mentors used to ask him, 'Damn it, Salk, why do you always do things differently?'

"Salk saw incongruities where others saw order. He learned expertise and questioned it at the same time—questioning not strong enough to prevent learning but strong enough to see opportunities to create new knowledge.

"Leonardo da Vinci also was a healthy skeptic. The most frequent words in his journals are 'I question.' He learned from the giants of the past but he questioned them and himself as well. He accepted nothing blindly. Likewise, Galileo never took anything for granted. He once said, 'In questions of science, the authority of a thousand is not worth the humble reasoning of a single individual.'"

Leonardo da Vinci

Challenge Assumptions and Rules

"Let me tell you one of my favorite stories," Marcus said. "Many automobile-racing rules were rewritten over the years because the Penske Race Team challenged them. For example, because many auto races are won by differences of seconds, shaving time from pit stops is a valuable endeavor. On one occasion, Penske's team members were trying to shave time from the thirteen seconds it took to refuel during a pit stop. They knew they could increase the flow rate by increasing the fueling pressure, but pumps were illegal under the rules of the racing association. So, with the help of Sun Oil engineers, they constructed a twenty-foot tower with a large gas tank on top of it and with a large fuel hose hanging from it. When a car drove in for refueling, they put the fuel hose in the tank, opened a valve on the fuel line, and filled the car's tank in three and one-half seconds. It was so dramatic that driver Mark Donohue said he felt the back of the car suddenly sink as the fuel poured in.

"But, within two races, the SCCA had rewritten the rules to outlaw the Penske invention. To Penske's opponents, the rules were the rules; the Penske team saw them as boundaries to be pushed. They asked, 'What don't the rules say?' The Penske team followed the first rule of innovation: there are no absolute rules."

"Are you a race fan?" I asked.

"No," he replied. "But I have an interest in what makes a Penske team able to win the Indianapolis Five Hundred twelve times—a record. And if racing were my chosen work, I would want to work on Penske's team to learn how to be a racing expert."

Create a Life That Is a Creative Journey to the Very End

"Researcher Mihalyi Csikszentmahalyi[39] says that creative people create their own lives. Their opportunity finding and seizing usually is rewarded, and their services are increasingly in demand. Their influence expands, leading to a wider set of opportunities. Csikszentmahalyi says they often create other sides of their personalities if that is needed to accomplish their goals. He says they learn to be objective or passionate or both. They can be imaginative and rooted in reality. When they don't have the expertise needed, they collaborate with others who have it."

Marcus shifted in his seat. "Creative people often create to the very end. Eight days before he died at the age of eighty-eight, Michelangelo was working on the Rondanini Pieta, a radical new work based on an entirely new concept. Pablo Casals, the great Spanish cellist, was developing and practicing a new piece of music on the day he died at the age of ninety-seven. Years after Marie Curie won a Nobel Prize, she was still creating."

Create Like a Child, Persevere Like a Soldier

"Creativity is a tightrope," he said. "We must be as free as children to create and, at the same time, we must discipline our minds. Beethoven expressed it well when he said, 'To make music, one must have the spirit of a gypsy and the discipline of a soldier.' The same is true for corporations; a Stanford University research team concluded from its study of public corporations of the nineteen eighties and nineteen nineties that corporations with the largest performance improvements developed the cultures of entrepreneurs and the discipline of soldiers[40]."

I asked, "You're saying that we must be somewhat childlike to be creative?"

"Yes," Marcus replied, "but we must also have disciplined focus. Have you watched small children at play? Mostly, they do what's fun. When it becomes difficult, they get frustrated and begin something else. Most children are playful, curious, and full of energy, but easily distracted. They do what gives them pleasure or satisfies their curiosity. The great innovators had fun and satisfied their curiosity while, at the same time, focusing energetically where their efforts would produce high returns. And, unlike children—who quit when the activity becomes difficult or unpleasant, they persevered."

Leverage Risk with Expertise

"Each time Curie discovered new knowledge, she saw more clearly the potential of her opportunity and she increased the amount of time and energy she applied. This is not risk taking; it is expert risk taking. What Curie did would be a waste of time for anyone without her expertise.

"When the great ones didn't have the expertise they needed in their work and when they knew they would dilute their efforts by taking the time to learn it, they leveraged their risk by teaming with others who had the expertise. Steve Jobs had marketing expertise, and Steve Wosniak had expertise in using microprocessors and in creating small computer hardware. They teamed up to create Apple Computer Corporation. Gates and Allen, Hewlett and Packard—these were great pairings because they took advantage of complimentary expertise."

The Creative Paradox

Marcus continued, "Throughout life, we have experiences that shape our attitudes, opinions, beliefs, and standards. We learn architectures, patterns, processes, and representations and store them in our brains. On the plus side, these help us to automatically drive to work, organize plans, and disassemble engines. They allow us to make many simple decisions and judgments without lengthy study. These patterns and principles are the sources of our creativity.

"On the negative side, these fixed ways of thinking can imprison our creativity and close our windows to opportunity. We may limit the options we see, filtering anything that doesn't 'fit.' Even the great ones sometimes closed their minds to opportunity. Thomas Edison and Bill Gates provide examples of this. While the rest of the world converted to alternating current, because it could be generated at low cost in large power stations and transmitted long distances efficiently, Edison opposed it. Later, after the world passed him by, Edison admitted that he was wrong."

"Initially, Bill Gates wouldn't invest in Internet software because he couldn't see how he'd ever get the money back from a free network. However, when he saw that the Internet was bearing down on Microsoft like a freight train, he admitted that he was wrong and began a major effort to build Internet support into the company's software and to establish Microsoft on the Internet."

"When the world changes and we continue to use models that are slow, error prone, costly, and inflexible, we become victims of our own expertise."

"Great innovators refuse to be stopped by fixed ideas. When Fred Smith started FedEx, Federal law prohibited his company from carrying loads on his planes that were large enough to make money. He persuaded the government that allowing him to carry larger loads would increase competition, thus benefiting the consumer. The government changed the law, against the protests of the major airlines."

"So we have a creative paradox," Marcus said. "No significant new achievement is possible without stored expertise, nor is it possible without going beyond existing expertise."

"We also must get beyond any limiting beliefs we may have."

Finding and Changing Limiting Thoughts

"Mike, have you ever had what you thought was a great idea but then immediately put it aside, thinking 'Somebody has probably already thought of that' or 'It's too big for me to pull off' or 'Nobody will listen to such a crazy idea'?

"About twenty years ago, Judy Anderson[41] had a great idea for starting her own business. She believed that name badges could be powerful marketing tools if they projected the right images in people's minds. She decided to quit her job and focus on her goal. She identified retail businesses for which she thought creative name badges would have large impacts. Then she designed and sent samples of name badges that would enhance their images with customers to these businesses.

"Months went by with no responses. Finally when Judy was out of money and her credit cards were at their limits, she received a call.

Judy Anderson

'How are you?' a deep voice asked. 'This is Sam Walton. I have your samples on my desk and I like your work. But it's not what I'm looking for.' Judy swallowed and said, 'Mr. Walton, what do you want to say to your customers when they walk through the door?' Sam replied, 'I want our customers to know that our people make the difference and that you can trust us on a handshake, and I want to have Wal-Mart on the badge.'

"'I'll make some new samples and send them to you in a few days,' she said.

"Judy spent the rest of the day producing a variety of drawings with 'Our people make the difference' and the Wal-Mart logo. She shipped the samples overnight to Sam. He loved the samples and ordered two hundred eighty thousand badges. From that beginning, Judy's company, Identification Systems, has grown into the largest custom-badge manufacturer in the world."

"What if Judy had allowed limiting thoughts, such as 'Wal-Mart is too big; it won't even look at an idea from someone who isn't in the name badge business' or 'If I quit my job and I fail, I won't be able to get another job as good as the one I have'?"

"Good point," I said. "How do we know when we have thoughts that limit us?"

"It's difficult," Marcus replied. "Most of the time, we're not aware of our limiting beliefs. An expert in behavioral change, who helps a person or organization find and change limiting beliefs, will begin with an analysis of recent unsatisfactory performance, lack of success, and/or unhappiness. The expert will try to determine if a limiting belief was the cause. When a limiting belief is identified, the expert helps the client to recognize situations in which that belief comes into play. Then the client is asked to rethink the reactions that led to failure and to create new positive responses."

"Sometimes our beliefs limit our ability to see future threats as well as opportunities. Unless we can identify and change our reactions, we'll be limited."

Creative Organizations

"Creative organizations usually are founded and led by creative individuals who have all the attitudes and behaviors we've just discussed and a few more," he said. "They are disciplined yet entrepreneurial.[42] The leaders of these organizations encourage open exchanges of ideas, yet they ask everyone to rally behind the opportunities that are selected for action. They set expectations of high creativity."

Creating Responsibly

I said, "Theodore Levitt,[43] a Professor Emeritus at Harvard Business School, says that ideas are useless unless implemented. So it is not enough just to come up with novel ideas. Each person who comes up with a new idea should first understand that the leaders of organizations continually are bombarded with problems and may not welcome new ideas. Second, in presenting the idea, the person should include at least a minimal indication of what it involves in terms of costs, risks, manpower, time, and perhaps even specific people to carry it through. He says that this is responsible behavior, because it is easier for the executive to evaluate the idea, which increases the chances that the idea will be used."

Marcus nodded in agreement, then glanced at his watch and stood. "We can go on to the Academia now," he said. After leaving the café, we turned at the corner on the west side of the Duomo and then walked north on Via Ricasoli. As we walked, he continued talking.

"In addition to developing their creative behaviors, the masters developed their visioning abilities, which enabled them to see and create the future. Our next master anticipated what large numbers of people would want in the future and led his company to create a whole new business," he said.

How Can We See Into The Future?

"In February, nineteen seventy-nine, the aging honorary chairman of Sony Corporation,[44] Masaru Ibuka, asked the product-development department to build a small tape player so that he could listen to stereo recordings on long flights. The engineers modified a small tape recorder, adding stereo circuitry. When they connected it to earphones, they were surprised. Instead of a small, narrow-band sound, the sound was full and wrapped itself around the listener.

"Two weeks later, Ibuka carried it on a flight and was delighted with the sound. When he returned, he gave it to the acting chairman, Akio Morita, who took it home for the weekend. That Saturday evening, as Morita entertained guests for dinner, he passed the player around and invited everyone to try it. Morita laughed as each guest showed amazement."

"Morita presented the player at the next executive meeting. The executives considered it a toy, so it shocked them when Morita proposed that they have it ready for sale in four months, at a time when students went on vacation. He set the price at one hundred twenty-five dollars. Morita was so enthusiastic and certain about it that the other executives reluctantly went along with his 'crazy idea.'

"Sony's engineers said that they would have to manufacture thirty thousand units per month to make a profit at a price of one hundred twenty-five dollars. The salespeople argued that they sold only fifteen thousand units per month of Sony's most popular tape recorder and that they could never sell a tape player that didn't record. Morita persisted and said that he would resign as chairman if the thirty thousand units didn't sell. He believed that many people would buy something they could listen to privately and while running or exercising.

"They named the new tape player the Walkman. For a month after the Walkman hit the market, there were no sales, which confirmed the predictions of the sales department. Then the sales began; there were thirty thousand in the next thirty days. The Walkman made Sony a world leader."

About six blocks north on Via Ricasoli, we stopped at the entrance to #60. "Before we go in, I'll begin to talk about seeing into the future. People who see into the future:
- Base their thinking outside the box on expertise inside the box
- Analyze trends, create future needs, and set high goals.
- Never say it can't be done."

Base Your Thinking Outside the Box on Expertise Inside the Box

"We have to go back twenty-five years to understand why the Walkman breakthrough was based on expertise inside the box," Marcus explained. "In nineteen fifty-three, when Ibuka heard that Bell Labs had invented the transistor, he realized that transistors would revolutionize electronics. So he sent Morita to America to purchase a license from AT&T to manufacture them. With the transistor, Sony produced the first handheld radio and led the world in miniaturization of radio products. By the time Morita had his vision for the Walkman, Sony had hired people who had expertise in miniature circuitry and had the capacity to build thousands of miniature tape recorders and radios. Sony was able to move quickly to dominate the portable tape-player market because it had the engineering, manufacturing, marketing, and distribution expertise to do so. Morita didn't create the Walkman; his organization did."

"Thinking outside the box begins with concepts, patterns, principles, and processes inside the box. Excuse my English, but out-of-the-box ideas like electric lamps, relativity, and the Walkman don't come from nothing. All the mind-freeing, brainstorming, and radical thinking won't get us out of the box with a great opportunity if we don't have expertise inside the box to bring ideas to fruition."

Analyze Trends, Create Future Needs, and Set High Goals

"Peter Drucker once said, 'The best way to predict the future is to create it.'[45] Predicting opportunities is a key to creating the future, for both individuals and organizations. Organizations can analyze where their competitors are making large profits and they can search for markets their competitors are not serving or that they are serving but would not likely defend. They can study changes in customer behavior that could be opportunities. They then can create visions to take advantage of the identified opportunities."

"There was no explicit customer need for the Walkman until Morita introduced it. People thought they needed it only after they saw it. Morita created a need. Many needs that we take for granted today were not obvious in their time. When presented with Alexander Graham Bell's telephone, U.S. President Rutherford B. Hayes said, 'It's a great invention, but who would want to use it anyway?' In nineteen thirty-six, *Radio Times* editor Rex Lambert said, 'Television won't matter in your lifetime or mine.' Sixteen years later, television was a major media player."

Never Say It Can't Be Done

Marcus leaned against the building. "In seventeen fourteen, after a fleet of British ships was sunk as a result of a navigational error, the British Board of Longitude offered a reward of twenty thousand pounds (over one million dollars in today's money) to anyone who could invent a method to measure longitude while on a ship at sea. The greatest scientist of all time, Isaac Newton, emphatically stated that no clock could be invented that could keep time precisely enough to do the job and that the only way to do it was with an astronomical instrument. Forty-five years later, John Harrison invented a type of clock called a chronometer. It wasn't an astronomical instrument but it measured time so accurately that it became the standard for longitudinal measurement for two centuries—until satellite global positioning systems were invented."

How Can We Visualize Great Opportunities?

Marcus said, "The great innovators visualize opportunities that others don't see because they:

- Focus on opportunities first, then creatively solve problems
- Sometimes set obviously unattainable goals
- Find new opportunities through creative synergies
- Prepare well for a breakthrough
- Incubate ideas."

Focus on Opportunities First, Then Creatively Solve Problems

"It's important, before we go further, to understand the difference between opportunities and problems. Jonas Salk creatively solved the problem of polio, a disease that crippled and killed people. But Sam Walton, Thomas Edison, Bill Gates, Akio Morita, Marie Curie, and Harland Sanders weren't solving problems; they were finding opportunities. Walton recognized that many consumers were attracted to lower-priced merchandise. Edison knew that offices and homes would want safe, practical lighting. Gates saw a computer on every desktop, running his software. Morita envisioned students carrying their own music and privately listening to it. Curie knew that science would advance if the source of the mysterious rays were discovered. Sanders knew he had a great fried-chicken recipe. Each of them first found an opportunity and then solved the problems that stood in the way of seizing it."

"When Marie Curie found the opportunity to discover a new element, she was faced with many problems. Great quantities of radioactive ore had to be acquired. Chemical processes to separate the compounds and a device to measure low-level radioactivity had to be invented. After Gates and Allen found the opportunity to create software for a personal computer, they had to solve hundreds of problems before they could seize it. After Morita found the opportunity to provide mobile entertainment for people, his company had to solve many problems in order to seize the opportunity."

"These innovators searched for and found opportunities first; then identified the problems—the barriers or obstacles—that needed to be surmounted in order to seize the opportunities; then focused their time, brainpower, and resources on solving the problems that stood in the way of seizing the opportunities.[49] When we find an opportunity and compare it to the way things currently are, we discover problems that must be solved creatively in order to seize the opportunity."

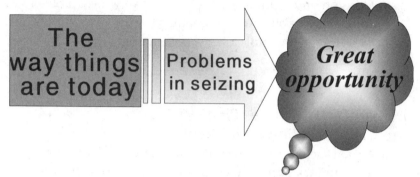

Find a great opportunity first, then solve the problems that prevent you from seizing it.

I said, "But many people say that necessity is the mother of invention. They say that you should look for the greatest pain or need that people have."

"Necessity is a mother of invention," Marcus said, "but it is not the only mother. True, Salk solved the problem of pain and death from polio. But was it necessary for Walton to offer discounts, for Morita to produce a Walkman, or for Curie to find radium? You could argue that Gates filled a need for a few eager computer enthusiasts, but most people didn't have the need until they saw what the software could do for them. If we simply solve the problems presented to us or try to find problems to solve, we will miss many great opportunities."

"I get your point. So you're saying that, if a person doesn't have enough problems, he or she should find an opportunity," I said, smiling.

Marcus almost cracked a smile before he plowed on. "The point is: Always focus on finding high leverage opportunities, then use creative problem-solving techniques to seize the opportunities. I won't discuss creative problem-solving techniques, because they are covered in many books,[46] and I'm sure you know them well. I put many of these techniques on my website: seeingdavidinthestone.com."

Breakthrough Opportunities

"Searching for and finding breakthrough opportunities is the highest form of visioning," he said. Breakthrough visions—like the printing press, the steam engine, wireless communication, penicillin, the transistor, the computer, and the Internet—changed the world. It's important to know how to find breakthrough opportunities so we can make jumps in progress that leave others behind. More than any other great one, Michelangelo helped our team understand the nature of breakthrough visioning. It's time to see his works."

As we entered the Academia, I caught the odor of aged wood and tapestries. I followed Marcus through an antechamber into a long, wide hall. A soft chill moved up my back as we entered the hallway. On each side,

Slave

white marble bodies of half-carved men appeared to struggle to get out of the stone that held them. At the end of the hallway, standing majestically in a stream of light from a skylight, was 'David.'

Marcus whispered, "These half-carved men are called 'The Slaves.' They show Michelangelo's remarkable expertise. Before he began to carve, he was able to see the finished form inside the stone."[47]

"Why didn't he finish them?" I asked

"Note that there are finely finished parts," he said. "Master sculptors say that Michelangelo wouldn't have finely finished some parts and left others rough unless he intended to. Maybe he wanted to show us in our personal prisons."

We walked down the hall toward the fourteen-foot-tall David. Marcus spoke quietly, his words echoing in the vaulted room. "The Florence Board of Works gave Michelangelo a seventeen-foot block of white marble that was so thin and so badly gouged by a previous artist that no one wanted it."

"All prior masters sculpted David 'after the battle,' with one foot placed triumphantly on Goliath's severed head. Michelangelo didn't believe that standing triumphant over a dead enemy was the essence of a great man. Instead, he portrayed David moments before the battle,

David, by Michelangelo

as he studied the enemy, dealt with his fears, and focused his mind and body."

I looked up in awe at the towering giant. His brow was furrowed with resolution, his eyes shooting like daggers. I could hear myself breathe.

Seeing David in the Stone

Marcus walked me over to one side and spoke quietly. "Michelangelo had an extraordinary ability. First, he was able to see in his mind a David capable of slaying Goliath. Second, he was able to see clearly the completed David in the damaged stone before he began to carve. Finally, he saw how to remove the excess stone to free David. Mike, in addition to identifying the timeless actions of the great ones, it's important to understand this almost mystical ability they had. They first saw or imagined the highest potential for themselves, others, and organizations. Then they saw where that high potential existed inside imperfect individuals and organizations. Finally, they knew how to help others and organizations to reach their highest potential."

Sometimes Set Obviously Unattainable Goals

"Les Wexner,[48] a retail pioneer and founder of The Limited clothing stores, uses visioning techniques and obviously unattainable goals to push others outside normal ways of thinking. Once, while discussing the marketing of a Shetland sweater that was projected to sell two hundred fifty thousand units, Les said to his staff of retailing experts, 'Humor me for just a minute. How would we sell a million sweaters?' Everyone in

Head of David

the room insisted that there was 'no way.' The Limited had eighty stores and would have to sell an average of twelve thousand five hundred sweaters per store. Les listened to the objections and then said, 'Just pretend. What would it take?'

"Then the team members formed mental images of selling a million sweaters, which would require a bigger resource base, more manufacturing plants, more colors in the assortment, a buy-one-get-one-free offer, incentives for stores, and so on. By implementing many of these ideas, they sold seven hundred fifty thousand Shetland sweaters—three times the original projection."

"Wexner knew that you can stimulate people's ability to create visions with questions such as: 'What would you do if you had the power to make anything happen that you wanted to happen?' 'What would magic look like?' 'What would the ideal solution be?' 'What if?' 'Why?' 'Why not?' 'If you had a wish . . . ?' 'What will it take to make us great?' Our imaginations are stretched by setting obviously unattainable goals, like Wexner's goal to sell sweaters. If goals are set so high that normal means can't achieve them, and if they're taken seriously by organizations that have the expertise, a breakthrough vision often appears."

Find New Opportunities Through Creative Synergies

"The story of Wexner's team also demonstrates the value of synergy in the creation process," Marcus said. "The team had a great deal of expertise inside each member's head. During the brainstorming and imaging sessions, each person's ideas stimulated ideas from others, and new combinations of ideas were formed. Wexner led the team members to create big mental images that were greater than the sum of the expertise stored in their individual minds. In other words, he led them to find new opportunity through creative synergy. Brainstorming is most effective when it is done in the pursuit of an opportunity, like 'selling a million sweaters.'"

Prepare Well for a Breakthrough

"On a chilly evening in eighteen sixty-five," Marcus began, "a Flemish chemist, Fredrich Kekulé, watched the patterns of flying sparks in his fireplace. As he slipped into half-sleep, he imagined that the sparks were linked in a circle, like snakes biting their own tails. He woke with a picture of hydrogen and carbon atoms in a ring and realized that this was a likely molecular structure for benzene. Other scientists finally accepted his description of the Benzene structure many decades after his death. People who write about creativity often use Kekulé's vision to show that visions happen like a magician's 'poof.' But, actually, the moment of illumination comes only after long-term preparation and incubation.[49] Before Kekule saw the Benzene ring in the fire, he was a professor of chemistry for nine years. He had extensive expertise in atomic-bonding principles and the patterns of chemical compounds.

"There also is a period of intense, short-term preparation in the days, weeks, and months preceding the breakthrough. During this period, the focus is usually narrowed to a specific area of opportunity, such as Curie's focus on finding radium and Edison's focus on a practical filament. So the lesson is: prepare well if you want a 'poof.'

"In summary, during long-term preparation, the mind is stocked with work expertise and opportunity-finding expertise. During short-term preparation, the specific area of opportunity is deeply studied and analyzed."

Incubate Ideas

"Incubation is a period of time in which an intent or goal in an area of opportunity percolates with all the long-term and short-term expertise stored in the subconscious. Breakthroughs often are described by their creators as mental images that occur after periods of incubation. Einstein imagined that he was riding on a beam of light and asked: If he were going at the speed of light, would the light reflected from his face be able to get back to him so that he could see himself in a mirror? His answer led to his theory of relativity. Beethoven once said, 'I always have a picture in mind when I'm composing.'

"Scientists say that we don't see the world around us as it is. Instead, we take the pieces that our optical systems collect and create images with them. We all have the mystical ability to create images. The *American Heritage Dictionary* defines 'vision' as 'a mental image produced by the imagination'; it defines 'imagine' as 'to form a mental picture or image'; and it defines 'see' as 'to have a mental image of, to visualize, to understand.' All these definitions are related to our abilities to create mental images. So if we want to improve our chances of creating breakthroughs, we should improve our abilities to create mental images."

Marcus started to move toward the door, then paused and looked back at David. "Once we creatively percolate the potential opportunities in our minds, illumination often occurs when we're not directly trying to see. It usually happens when we're at the edge of consciousness, in a near-dream state. It's as if the goal becomes a spotlight, sweeping through the caves of our unconscious minds, locating and combining bits and scraps until it finds answers. Often, after long deliberation, insights occur suddenly when we're not consciously searching. An insight may occur in the midst of a long drive or walk, in the shower or bath, or on a vacation. The insights come to the surface because reducing signal levels to our brains through relaxation increases our access to our subconscious minds. That's why creative people get away from the quest and do something relaxing or diversionary."

"Einstein's sister said that, when he had a deep physics problem on his mind, he'd play the violin. Often, while playing his violin, he'd suddenly come to a stop and declare, 'Now I've got it.' Edison and Einstein used the same trick to access the subconscious. After percolating a problem in his mind for a while, each would sit in a chair with his hands hanging down, holding balls or rocks. When he dozed and dropped a ball or rock, he'd jot down the first ideas that came to him. Of course, each person must search for ways that work for him or her. Keep in mind that the incubation phase will not produce a vision without the expertise that comes from good preparation and good goal focus."

Opportunity-Visioning Games

"Marcus," I cut in, "some people believe that breakthroughs only come from a few gifted minds and magicians like you."

"I don't create opportunities!" he protested. "I help people with expertise to find them. Sometimes I use realistic games and simulations to help people imagine what is possible[50] or to see their Davids in the stone. I have many examples on my website: seeingdavidinthestone.com

Going Beyond Fear

Marcus looked back at David again. "Michelangelo saw all that David could be in that damaged block of stone. The giant Goliath had challenged David's people to choose a man to fight him. If the man they chose killed him, the Philistines would accept defeat and become

Michelangelo

subjects. But if Goliath killed the man, David's people would be their slaves." He turned to me and said quietly, "To me, David represents everyone who goes beyond fear, who pursues a higher mission, who puts the interests of others first. David also is an inspiration to us to search for our Davids in the stone or to help other people and organizations to see theirs."

On the way out of the Academia, Marcus stopped at a bronze sculpture of Michelangelo. It was finely carved, showing his intensity and his sad, knowing eyes. "It's hard to relate to a genius who lived in poverty," I said.

Marcus shot me an incredulous look. "Fairy tales!" he said. "Michelangelo headed an art enterprise that pre-sold its work and profited over thirty million dollars in today's money in his lifetime.[51] [52] He was a businessman who chose to live frugally when he became rich. He cared more for his work."

"I didn't know that," I said.

We headed south when we left the Academia. Marcus said, "Once we have honed our knowledge and skills through experience and have developed our visioning techniques, we and our organizations will find many opportunities. To maximize our chances of success, we need ways to sort out and choose only the opportunities that will produce very high value for the time, effort, and resources required to find and seize them. I call these 'high-leverage opportunities.' This is the next creative action of the great ones. Our next master knew how to choose."

ACTION 4.

Select Only High-Leverage Opportunity

My job is to put the best people on the biggest opportunities and the best allocation of dollars in the right places.

Jack Welch[53]

"One day, on her lunch hour," Marcus began, "Cheryl Krueger was walking in Manhattan when she saw a line of people wrapped around a street corner. The line ended at David's Cookies, which was selling lumpy, moist, delicious cookies reminiscent of her grandmother's."

"Cheryl had learned from her grandma how to make such cookies, so when she discovered that David's was selling franchises, she arranged to meet the owner. In a twenty-minute meeting, she discovered that he wanted a franchise fee of two hundred fifty thousand dollars as well as ten percent of the gross and that Cheryl would have to buy all her cookie dough from him and pay for the shipping."

"On the plane back to Columbus, Ohio, her home town, Cheryl pictured the people standing in line. The cookie business would give her control of her life, but, after a hard analysis of the numbers, she calculated that she would have to sell a million dollars worth of cookies per year in order to make a profit. She began to wonder what she would be getting for the franchise costs. From her creative marketing expertise came the question: Did the name David's Cookies mean anything in Columbus? Cheryl spent her weekend asking people if David's Cookies meant anything to them. None of them knew the name."

"So Cheryl created a business plan of her own and approached the banks. The banks asked why people would buy cookies when they could bake them. Cheryl told them that many women were busy with careers and weren't baking much anymore. When the banks turned her down, she decided to finance the business herself.

"For three years after she opened her first store, Cheryl continued working in New York as a clothing-company executive. Each Friday, she flew to Columbus, worked in her store over the weekend, and returned to New York on an early Monday-morning flight. When the first store could support her, she quit her executive job and opened a second store."

Cheryl Krueger

"As the number of stores increased, Cheryl found a valuable opportunity to create a central baking operation to supply all the stores. That led to another opportunity. The retail dessert business was highly seasonal, and Cheryl did not like to lay off employees during the off-peak periods in her bakery. So, to level out her bakery orders, she sold private-label desserts to businesses that served desserts all year long, such as Bob Evans, Ruby Tuesday's, and Max & Erma's. Then a few travel agencies began giving Cheryl's cookies to airline representatives. The airlines liked the cookies and asked Cheryl to wrap them individually for their passengers. Today, her company supplies cookies to Delta, US Air, The Limited, and The Walt Disney Company. When Hallmark decided to become the premier gift company, it not only chose Cheryl&Co as its dessert supplier, it took a minority interest in her company. Using her expertise and her ability to select only the most valuable opportunities, Cheryl built Cheryl&Co into a successful, multimillion-dollar enterprise.

"To understand how people like Cheryl sort great opportunities from poor ones," Marcus said, "we need to answer three questions:
- How do we select high-leverage opportunities?
- How do we eliminate low-leverage or wasteful activity?
- How do we eliminate the cost of lost opportunity?"

"Let's begin with the first question."

4. Select only high-leverage opportunities
- How do we select high-leverage opportunities?
- How do we eliminate low-leverage or wasteful activity?
- How do we eliminate the cost of lost opportunity?

How Do We Select High-leverage Opportunities?

"Cheryl knew the difference between a poor opportunity and a great one because of her extensive expertise and her high-leverage thinking. She had learned about purchasing and the art of negotiation as an assistant buyer at Burdines Department Store. She learned retail merchandising and management during four years as merchandising manager at The Limited. She gained business experience as an assistant vice president with Claus Sportswear. Before she started her own retailing business, she knew how to prove that something would sell at a price, that it could be purchased at the right price and quality, and that it would sell for a profit. She knew how things were made, distributed, promoted, and sold. She knew how to realistically forecast, survey, estimate, and analyze the likely success of an opportunity."

"Many who see an opportunity and take the risk fail because they see only the benefits and they underestimate the costs of seizing the opportunity. Cheryl says, 'What separates a winner from a loser is the ability to be realistic, to do the hard numbers, to be as tough with themselves as a boss would be. And it's easier to be realistic when it's your own money at risk.'[54] There are many opportunities to be found. However, before deciding to seize an opportunity, successful people and successful businesses try to predict how much long-term benefit they would get from it compared to the time, brainpower, and other resources they would have to spend to seize it."

"To select only great opportunities, you must first determine if the opportunity is one of the best opportunities to meet your long-term goals. Second, you must calculate the overall value of the opportunity. The overall value of an opportunity is the expected future benefits of the opportunity minus the costs of seizing it. For example, Cheryl expected to create a long-term business that she would love to do and that would provide her with a lifetime of earnings. For that, she was willing to sacrifice a number of years in the beginning, when she put her time and money into the business but had no returns."

"To calculate future benefits, risk must be considered. If the opportunity has only a fifty-fifty chance of success, the expected future benefits are cut in half."

"Even if the opportunity is a very good fit with your long-terms goals, and its overall value is high, it may not be the best opportunity to invest your resources in. Another calculation is needed to find the best opportunity.

> The overall value of an opportunity is the expected future benefits of the opportunity minus the costs of seizing it.

"Thinkers like Cheryl get an expectation of the return they'll get on the resources they invest by dividing the expected future benefits by the resources required to seize the benefits. Expected future benefits include increased value and contribution to long-term strategy, money, or whatever the seizer considers valuable. Resources include time, money, effort, and whatever is required to seize the benefits."

Short-term Versus Long-term Thinking

"Many people want short-term payoffs," he said. "They won't devote time to preparation, because it doesn't pay off immediately. Since the great achievers knew the long-term value of preparation, they spent their time, thoughts, and resources on activities that had the best combination of short-term and long-term returns."

"In my early years at Dardenn," I said, "Jesse Dardenn didn't always have the money to pay me, so he gave me stock instead. I had to moonlight to pay the bills. Later, when the company was doing well, he offered to buy back my stock. I was willing to sell it, but my wife Ellie convinced me to keep it. She said that Jesse and I were building something that would be worth a lot someday. She was thinking of the long term."

"Ellie was a wise woman," Marcus said. "I was very sorry when she passed away."

"I'm just getting used to the idea that she's gone," I said. "I spend more time at the office now."

How Do We Eliminate Low-leverage Or Wasteful Activity?

Marcus nodded. "The great achievers knew that most activities, events, and transactions in life are wasteful. Darwin Smith, the CEO of Kimberly-Clark,[55] concluded that annual forecasts of earnings, a Wall Street tradition, focused too much on the short term and provided no real value to stockholders, so he stopped doing them. He also eliminated titles and management layers before the idea was popular. Under Smith, Kimberly-Clark's stock outperformed those of the other best paper-products companies by four to one."

"So, before committing resources to seize opportunities, the great achievers made sure that the opportunities were the highest-leverage ones they could find. They all asked some questions to increase their chances of success, such as:

- Is this opportunity the largest benefit we can get from our resources?
- Is it worth far more than the time, effort, and resources needed to achieve it?
- Is it practical?
- Can it be done?
- Is it a source of passion for us?"

"As we discussed before, to produce the best results, more resources should be focused on opportunities than on problems," he said. "The great ones knew both where and how to focus resources and where not to focus them. Even when we decide to focus resources on high-leverage opportunities, we can't do it if wasteful activity fills the day."

Guideline for Determining If an Activity Is Wasteful

I asked, "Do you have a set of guidelines for identifying wasteful activity?"

He replied, "The most important guideline is: if you haven't analyzed an activity and determined whether it is high-leverage, it's probably wasteful. It's also probably wasteful if you do it routinely without thinking about it. For example, if you do it just because it's a problem or a nagging concern; because it's in your mail, e-mail, or phone messages; because it's traditional or habitual; because it's the first solution that pops up; because it's a policy without regard for benefit or cost; because it's a regular meeting; because it's the popular thing to do; or because it's a solution that always worked in the past."

"You've heard people say, 'I'm keeping busy.' Keeping busy, being active, and 'getting things done' pleases many people. However, we should heed the advice of the great basketball coach, John Wooden, who said that we must not mistake activity for achievement."

"The goal is to pick opportunities that best fit your long-term strategic goals and also have both high, overall value and a high return on the investments of time, brainpower, and resources. Furthermore, as a person gains greater responsibility and influence, he or she should choose opportunities that also have higher overall value."

"People and organizations don't intentionally waste resources on low-benefit, high-cost activities," I said.

"True," he agreed, "but if they don't focus on high-leverage opportunities, they naturally drift toward lower ones, which are easier to find, more plentiful, and easier to implement."

We crossed the Ponte Vecchio, an ancient bridge lined on both sides with shops. I glanced to the west to see the sun shimmering on the

Ponte Vecchio Bridge

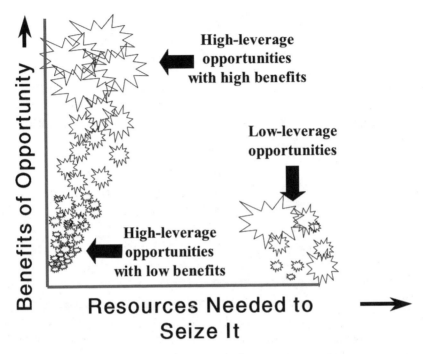

river. When we reached the south side of the river, Marcus stopped and opened the manuscript he was carrying. He turned to a page, which he showed to me. "In this drawing, I show that high-leverage opportunities come in all sizes, large and small."

"The larger the star in the drawing, the larger the opportunity. As I said before, the best leaders focus their time and resources on opportunities in the upper left side, where the long-term benefits are high and the time, brainpower, and resources needed to seize them are small, compared to the benefits. The best leaders don't support low-leverage activity."

Acceptable Opportunities

He continued, "There's a test I use before deciding to seize an opportunity. I estimate the lowest reasonable benefits to be expected from the opportunity. Then I divide the lowest reasonable benefits by an estimate of the highest reasonable costs to seize the benefits."

"Most people do the opposite," I said. "They calculate the most optimistic benefits with the least cost. Your test is a pessimistic approach."

"It depends on your expertise," he said. "If you're an expert-insider and can make good estimates of benefits and costs, an optimistic approach is okay. Risk and available resources also must be considered.

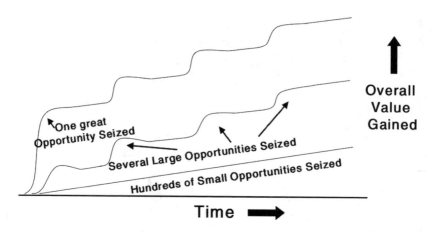

My test is a guideline, not a formula you can use without judgment."

Small Versus Large Improvement

I said, "Marcus, it sounds as if you're primarily focused on big opportunities. At Dardenn, we encourage people to find opportunities to make small improvements as well as large ones. A lot of small improvements can add up to big improvement over time."

He nodded. "That's true. I also encourage improvements of all sizes. Sometimes people misunderstand what I'm saying. I'm not just talking about great or large opportunities. Valuable opportunities come in all sizes. The smallest improvement is valuable if the long-term benefits are greater than the cost to seize the benefits."

He pointed to another drawing in the manuscript and said, "As you can see from the drawing, a lot of overall value can be gained from seizing many small opportunities. On the other hand, seizing a few large opportunities or even one great opportunity can produce the same overall value to a person or an organization. The highest-achieving organizations train their people to seize opportunities of all sizes so long as the value of the opportunities are larger than the time, effort, and resources required to seize them."

I asked, "Should every individual in an organization be trained to be a high-leverage thinker?"

"Yes," he replied, "because all wasteful activities, no matter how small or how large, drain the resources of individuals and organizations. They use up time and resources that would be better spent on valuable activities. The result is lost opportunity."

How Do We Eliminate The Cost Of Lost Opportunity?

"When we spend our time, brainpower, and resources on low-leverage activity, we lose the benefits we could have had if we had spent the time, brainpower, and resources on finding and seizing high-leverage opportunities. This is the cost of lost opportunity. If you are in an organization that has competitors, you and your organization fall behind when you lose opportunity."

"Every worthwhile activity can't easily be related to long-term benefits," I said. "For example, if someone proposes a small improvement that eliminates wasteful activity in an office procedure, it might not go directly to the bottom line. But by encouraging people to make those changes, you develop an organization that is always finding and seizing opportunity. Then, when you're ready to make large improvements, people are more willing. That's helped us make our goal of eight-percent productivity improvement per year. And a vision doesn't have to be on the scale of Curie's or Einstein's to be important. People at Dardenn make dozens of important but small contributions every day."

"I agree," he said. "Your productivity results are impressive. Earlier, I pointed out that research shows that when people or organizations like yours are in the process of preparing for, finding, and seizing opportunity, they learn at a higher rate and at a higher quality. And when they're performing all the actions of the great ones, they're on the path to greatness."

"How much time and activity should Dardenn invest in preparing for, finding, and seizing opportunity?" I asked.

"Dardenn's automatic valve market is fast-changing, so I believe you should spend at least twenty percent of your total time and activity. If you were in the semiconductor or telecommunications industry, I would increase that amount. If you were starting up a new business, it could be as high as eighty percent. The greater the speed of change in your market or the greater amount you must learn in a short time, the greater the time you should spend on finding and seizing opportunities."

He waited for my acknowledgment. I nodded my head, and he continued.

"We are on the path of the great ones if we are preparing for, finding, and seizing the most valuable opportunities, large or small, within our influence. The great ones searched until they were satisfied that they had found the highest-leverage opportunities within their areas.

Like mountain climbers, they searched through the clouds for the highest peaks."

"Mike," he continued, "what techniques do you use to find the most valuable opportunities?"

"I use the one Jesse Dardenn taught me," I answered. "When anyone proposed that we invest in a project, Jesse would always ask if we could think of any better opportunity. That always made us search for a higher peak."

"That's a good rule," he said.

Summary Of The Four Actions To Find Great Opportunity

"To summarize," he said, "first, the great ones differentiated themselves by choosing to search for opportunity where they had the best chances of finding great opportunity. Second, they became expertise-insiders by using powerful learning processes to learn the high-leverage expertise of their work. They adopted the most creative behaviors and learned to envision opportunities. Finally, they selected only opportunities that had high benefits compared to the time, brainpower, and resources they had to use to seize them."

Obtaining The Willing Support Of Others

We reached the street just outside the apartment where I was staying. Marcus said, "I have to leave you now, and I know you need to rest after your overnight trip. Before tomorrow, I'd like you to think about something. In all the cases we discussed today, opportunity finders and seizers—such as Edison, Curie, Walton, Krueger, and Gates—obtained the willing support of others when they were seizing. Our research findings were quite clear on how the great ones gathered the support of others and why many other opportunity finders stumbled or fell at this point.

"The best leaders studied how other great leaders multiplied themselves through others. They discovered four more actions. With these actions, they were able to mobilize the support they needed to seize opportunities. These are in the next section of the manuscript. Tomorrow, we'll explore the art and science of using these four actions."

"To prepare for tomorrow, imagine that you've found a great opportunity. However, to seize it, you need the time and resources of others, and those others are less than willing. I'll pick you up here at five-thirty a.m." He turned and disappeared around the corner.

Dardenn

There was another message on my cell phone from Paul, our engineering director. When I reached him, he began to talk rapidly. "Mike, Larry came to me and ordered me to change the drawings to remove the vent, I refused. He was furious."

The phone beeped. "A call's coming in," I said. "It's Ron; I'll get back to you."

"We've got a big problem here," Ron said in a parental tone. "Paul told Larry he won't change the drawings. Paul's making more money than he's worth and now he's telling us what he'll do and what he won't do ? You straighten him out or I will!" He hung up.

I called Paul and reminded him that the Darden boys owned the company and asked him if he could think of a way to stall them until I got back. He said he would try.

I also had a message from Mary Scott, Dardenn's chief financial officer. She said that the president of the bank had asked her to supply a profit-and-loss statement and a balance sheet. With our large cash reserves, no long-term debt, and no line of credit, she couldn't understand why the bank needed that information. She said that the officer at the bank wouldn't tell her why. I called her and left a voice message, saying that she shouldn't give them anything without Ron's okay.

I had an early dinner. There was still daylight when I fell into bed, exhausted. I tossed and turned that night. I wondered why, with so many great opportunities in the business, Larry had picked a negative opportunity as his first project. The lesson is: when you don't have expertise in the field, you are not prepared to identify high-leverage opportunities, much less to distinguish good ones from poor ones.

It amazed me that the first four actions of the great ones seemed to apply specifically to my problems at Dardenn. On the other hand, maybe those actions would apply to all situations involving problems and opportunities.

I was awakened by my alarm at four-fifty a.m. I showered, dressed, and walked downstairs to the street to wait for Marcus.

Mobilize Support

8. Find common meaning with and negotiate with opposers
7. Sell the opportunity to those that are cautious
6. Co-create with those eager for opportunity
5. Find the highest meanings of others

Find Great Opportunities

4. Select only high-leverage opportunities
3. Learn to envision opportunities
2. Use powerful learning processes
1. Differentiate yourself for opportunity

PART II

Four Actions to Mobilize Support

*Visions are never the sole property of one man or one woman.
Before a vision can become reality, it must be owned by every
single member of the group.*[56]

Phil Jackson, winner of nine NBA titles

A t five-thirty a.m., Marcus's car arrived in front of my apartment building, and I got in. As the driver pulled away from the curb, Marcus told me that we were headed for Carrara, in the Alpi Apuan Mountains.

Shortly after we left the city, he turned toward me again. "Last night, I asked you to imagine that you had found a great opportunity that you knew how to seize and that you needed the help of others to seize it. All the great ones needed the help of others to seize opportunities. Edison was always searching for financial investors for his projects. Michelangelo sought and received the patronage of many powerful people, including Lorenzo and Giuliano de' Medici and Pope Julius II."

"Although Bill Gates has outstanding technical aptitude, it's his ability to influence others to help him seize opportunities that has made him the leader of the personal-computer software revolution and the richest man in the world. By convincing IBM to buy nonexclusive rights to the operating system he developed for its personal computer, he was able to legally sell the same software to all the companies that cloned IBM's personal computer."

"The great opportunity seizers took the next four actions to influence others to invest their time, ideas, and resources:

5. Find the highest meanings of others
6. Co-create with those eager for opportunity
7. Sell the opportunity to those that are cautious
8. Find common meaning with and negotiate with opposers"

"In this way, they multiplied themselves through others. Action five, finding the highest meanings of others, is the foundation action for mobilizing support."

Find The Highest Meanings Of Others

Fail to honor people; they fail to honor you.

Lao-Tzu

"To find the highest meanings of others, we should know the answer to four questions:
- How do we gain the respect of others?
- How do we begin to involve others?
- How do we see opportunity from other's eyes?
- How do we find the high meanings that others will change for?

I'll address each of these questions."

How Do We Gain The Respect Of Others?

"When the great ones didn't respect the power of others, they paid a dear price—as our next visionary did," said Marcus. I'll begin his story in a courtroom years ago, as he was ushered in."

The Trial

"A bearded old man, he walked unsteadily, his deep-set eyes piercing the room. He was fearful. In his seventy years, he had never been on trial before. His doctors had told the court that he would die if removed from his sickbed, but the court had ordered him to appear anyway."

"The prosecutor, a thin, heavily wrinkled man, robed in red and purple, was seated at a small oak table. For him, this was a must-win trial. Far more was at stake than the crime; both the law and the system were on trial. The defendant had to be stopped. The prosecutor rose and, without facing the defendant, began his examination: 'Do you have anything to say?'[57]

Galileo

"The old man sighed deeply. 'I have nothing to say.' In contrast to his thin, clean-shaven opponents, the old man was a large, swarthy man with an immense beard and a bald head that stretched far behind a deeply furrowed forehead."

"The prosecutor narrowed his eyes as he turned toward the old man. 'Do you hold or have you held that the sun, not the earth, is the center of the universe?'

"The defendant knew what he had to say to save his life: 'I hold the opinion the earth is the center of the universe.'

"His thoughts drifted back to the beginning. It began when he built a telescope so powerful that he could see ships fifty miles out on the Aegean Sea. When he invited members of the Venetian Senate to look through his telescope, they were amazed. Overnight, the military and commercial world fell at his feet."

"The prosecutor scowled. He lifted a copy of the old man's book, *Dialogue,* from the table. 'Do you hold the opinion the earth goes around the sun?' He slammed the book to the table. 'Tell the truth!'

"'I did not write the book because I hold that opinion,' the old man replied.

"'I repeat. From the nature of the book, you have held the opinion the earth moves about the sun.' The prosecutor's voice rose to a shout. 'Tell the truth! Otherwise, we will torture!'

"The old man slumped in his chair. He knew that, a few years earlier, a Franciscan friar, Giordano Bruno, had been brutally tortured and then burned alive for heretical beliefs.

"'I am here to obey,' he said, with what appeared to be all his remaining strength.

"The old man's thoughts drifted again. If only he'd been content to view ships at sea, but he had improved his telescope until he could see what no one had ever seen: moons rotating around other planets. He remembered being frozen to the eyepiece. What he saw contradicted Aristotle's theory that all heavenly bodies rotated around the earth."

"The long silence in the courtroom ended when the prosecutor returned from his huddle with the Inquisitor. He said that the trial was over. The old man was led back to his cell."

"The next day, he knelt before his inquisitors and said in a weak voice, 'I, Galileo Galilei . . . swear that I've always believed, I believe now, and, with God's help, will always believe all that is held and preached by the Holy Catholic Church. . . .'"

"He was sentenced to house arrest for life and barred from ever expressing his views. He had to publicly apologize. His book was forbidden, and his condemnation read to professors and students of science in Italy."

"He was angry. Why had they done this to him? With his telescope, he had shown them that Jupiter had four moons circling it. He was sure that they'd marvel at the power of the creator. But they refused to 'see.' Eight years later, he died a prisoner in his villa in Arcetri, just up the hill from where you're staying. I'll leave a map for you."

Marcus became silent. Finally, I asked, "Is that all you have to say about Galileo?"

Marcus cocked his head to one side. "Did Galileo get a fair trial?" he asked.

"No," I said.

"Put yourself in the church's position," he said. "Suppose you believed that the splendor you saw above you on a dark night was heaven. Galileo was asking you to believe that you were seeing just more suns and planets."

"But his evidence was powerful," I protested.

"If Galileo were right, the earth would be revolving at one thousand miles per hour, and we'd be orbiting the sun at sixty-seven thousand miles per hour. The winds would blow us over, and we'd be flung off. A ball thrown into the air would not fall straight down. But we're not flung off, the winds don't blow us over, and a ball does fall straight down. It's obvious that we're standing still and that the heavens revolve about us."

"But wrong," I said.

"You'll never be able to lead where others can't lead until you learn to respect the expertise of those who have different views of the world," Marcus said.

"Are you saying that I should condone the view of the Church at that time?"

"Not condone! Respect! Appreciate! In his book, Galileo made fools of those who believed that the earth was the center of the universe. These included the Pope. A leader must have more than the truth; he must know how to help others see it. When some visionaries become frustrated with resisters, they attack them. They make war and they get war; there's a winner, there's a loser. And when they underestimate the relative power of the resisters, they're the losers."

"But ideas like Galileo's are always going to elicit opposition," I said.

"How controversial was the theory of evolution that Charles Darwin proposed?" he asked.

"Very controversial," I replied.

"But Darwin welcomed the challenges of others and openly questioned his own work. Darwin respected the power, expertise, and viewpoints of others. He, in turn, was so respected that many colleagues who disagreed with him did not attack him."

The Lesson of the Stone

Marcus stopped talking and looked out the window. As we rode along, I watched the Tuscan hills come to life in the predawn light and I dozed. I was shaken awake when we rolled onto a very rough road. The warm sun was coming through the window. I looked out to see that the world dropped hundreds of feet below us. We were winding along an eight-foot-wide road cut into a mountain. I was relieved when we stopped.

5. Find the highest meanings of others

- How do we gain the respect of others?
- How do we begin to involve others?
- How do we see opportunity from others' eyes?
- How do we find high meanings that others will change for?

"From here it's risky to drive," he said. I smiled, realizing that he thought the road to this point was safe. Picking up a backpack from the floor, he opened his door and stepped briskly into the morning sunlight, and I followed. After a short walk, we rounded a

Carrara marble quarry

turn, and a vast quarry of white stone opened below us. The mountain was terraced in building-block fashion, where large cubes of marble had been cut and removed. Marcus stopped. Reflections from the morning sun skipped across the mine.

"This is pure white marble, the finest in the world, preferred by Michelangelo," he said. "Mined here since the time of the Roman Empire." He removed a bottle from the side pocket of his backpack and splashed water onto the marble wall facing the inside of the road. Running his fingers along the wet, sparkling crystals, he said, "See the small lines of impurities as the crystals catch the light. This marble has the least impurities of all marble but even it will shatter if struck in the wrong place. It's unforgiving."

He pulled a pouch from his pocket and removed a piece of polished marble. He turned it over to a roughly cleaved side, where thousands of small crystals glistened. "I watched my mother sculpt the stone this came from," he said, handing me the piece. "One day, when she wasn't looking, I picked up her hammer and struck the stone. That piece broke off, and the sculpture was ruined. The stone didn't forgive my lack of expertise, but my mother did. She said I had learned the lesson of the stone.

"She showed me the imperfection that caused the stone to fracture when I struck it. She said that success comes from visualizing the final image inside the stone and knowing where to strike the stone so it will willingly yield the final image. She said that if I wanted to sculpt, she would teach me to see the image inside and also to see the imperfections in the stone."

"Michelangelo knew the lesson of the stone. His mother died when he was a baby, and he was sent to the wife of a stonecutter to be wet-nursed. All his life, Michelangelo remembered the reverence of the old stonecutters toward the stone and their mystical words of caution: 'The power lay in the stone, not in the arms or the tools. If ever a mason came to think he was master, the stone would oppose him.'[58]

"Later in my life," he said, "I realized that great leaders knew the lesson of the stone. They approached each new mission with the humility of a sculptor. They knew that if they put themselves above people, people would oppose them."

"I began to study great failures, such as Galileo's. People often failed because they thought they were superior; they didn't respect the expertise and power of those who opposed them. In the mid-eighteenth century, the King of England imposed stiff new taxes and laws on the American colonies without their consent. He thought they had no choice but to comply. You know the rest of the story."

"Great leaders mobilize support by first respecting the expertise and power of others."

I handed the piece of marble back to him. "Have you ever shattered the stone when you were working with a client?" I asked.

"Yes. Now I begin every opportunity search with a client by reminding myself that, as the sculptor respects the stone, great leaders know that power comes from those they lead."

How Do We Begin To Involve Others?

Marcus looked out at the mountain of white marble and said, "Leaders who don't see opportunity from the eyes of others make many common errors. The first error is to fail to identify and involve others early enough in the process. The second error is to not know or care about the needs and wants of others—as Galileo did. The third is to overestimate the acceptance of others, and the fourth is to underestimate the power of the opposition. To avoid common leadership errors:
- Identify and involve others early
- Know the needs and wants of others.
- Don't overestimate the acceptance of others
- Don't underestimate the power of the opposition

"I'll discuss each of these briefly."

Identify and Involve Others Early

"To identify whom to involve, a leader must imagine what the future will be like once the opportunity is seized. There are two groups of people that must be identified: those whose help is needed to seize the opportunity and those whose lives will be changed by seizing the opportunity. I have a checklist in the manuscript for identifying those who must be involved," he said. He pulled it out of his backpack, thumbed through it, and handed it to me.

Checklist of Those Who Should Be Involved Early

❑ *Who stands to gain the most from seizing this opportunity?*
❑ *Whose time, expertise, and resources are needed to seize the opportunity?*
❑ *Who are the power-insiders that must be involved to seize the opportunity?*
❑ *Who needs to change what they are doing to seize the opportunity?*
❑ *Which employees, customers, or suppliers will be affected significantly?*
❑ *Who will oppose the seizing of the opportunity?*

Know the Needs and Wants of Others

I handed the manuscript back to him, and he put it away. He began to walk, and I followed him up the marble mountain. "Even great ones sometimes lose sight of the needs and wants of others. Early in the twentieth century, Henry Ford's ability to see that customers wanted an affordable, durable automobile made him a giant in the automobile industry. But, in nineteen twenty-five, General Motors introduced car buyers to variety, style, yearly model changes, and purchase financing. At that time, Henry was out of touch with the needs and wants of his most important customers. He continued to build only one model and denounced financing as evil. By nineteen twenty-seven, Ford had lost most of its customers. After suffering huge losses and being threatened with ruin, Henry changed his mind and provided variety, model changes, and financing. Today Ford puts customers' needs first."

"Winning customers back was costly to Henry Ford. Research has shown that it's much more expensive to win a new customer than it is to keep an existing one. So it's important to know your customer's real wants and needs."

"I agree that knowing the needs and wants of others is good," I said, "but sometimes a leader should do what's right, no matter what others may think they need. In nineteen eighty-one, we were losing a half million dollars a month at Dardenn. I calculated that we'd save three hundred thousand a month by closing one plant and moving production and all the people to our main plant. Some people didn't want to move, but we made the decision. Shutting that plant down prevented a layoff."

"Did you present the financial situation to the affected employees before the move?"

"No, I thought it would worry them unnecessarily. I should have. Today, I would."

"Good," Marcus said. "The people still may not have liked it, but many would have understood that it was for the long-term benefit of them and the company."

Don't Overestimate the Acceptance of Others and Don't Underestimate the Power of the Opposition

"Great opportunity finders and seizers are energized by the visions they create and are stimulated by change," he said. "These are great strengths. On the other hand, they're sometimes so passionate, they can't see a vision through the eyes of those affected by the vision. For

example, Abraham Lincoln was a master in human relations but, during the Civil War, he had ex-congressman Clement Vallandigham jailed after an anti-war speech[59] and he revoked the writ of *habeas corpus* so that all critics of the war could be jailed indefinitely[60]. He then shut down the Chicago Times because of its antiwar views. All over the nation, speakers rose to condemn the arrests, the war, and an unjust draft that allowed the rich to hire people to take their places. In

President Abraham Lincoln

New York City, police and marines couldn't stop the mobs when they rioted against the draft. Hundreds were killed."

"Lincoln's staunchest supporters pleaded with him to back off. Lincoln, surprised by the reaction, freed the critics, allowed the *Times* to publish again, and reinstated the writ of *habeas corpus*. Even a great leader like Lincoln sometimes overestimated the acceptance of others."

"Some leaders leave the opposition out until they are sure they can seize the opportunity," he added.

I said, "I've done that, and all went well in the beginning. But when the opposition heard about it, they felt left out, and I lost their trust. They exaggerated rumors of changes and job cuts. I had a battle on my hands. Now I get everybody involved early."

"Good approach," he said. "Once we identify those that should be involved early, before we can get them to willingly invest their time, expertise, and resources, we must learn to see the opportunity the way they see it."

We continued to walk up the mountain. At one point, we rounded a corner and looked down on an active marble mine below us. "There may be no one who is better able to 'see what others see' than our next master," Marcus said.

How Can We See Opportunity From Others' Eyes?

"In nineteen seventy-six, the WJZ-TV newsroom in Baltimore received a call from a new reporter at the scene of a fire. The reporter said that the station should not do a story on the fire because it was too horrifying. The news desk ordered her to cover it. Obediently, she interviewed a woman who had lost seven children in the fire. She cried with the woman as the camera rolled.

"That evening, after the film was aired, the reporter apologized on the air for crying. Co-workers criticized both her loss of control and her apology as unprofessional. She was told that she didn't have the 'right stuff' for big-city reporting. The station gave her a second chance as a news co-anchor but quickly removed her.

"Then a new manager decided to create a morning talk show to run opposite the popular Donohue show. The ex-reporter was picked as co-host. The show was assessed as having a slim chance of success, but the ex-reporter had something the odds-makers didn't know about. She was a genius at finding the human-interest side of a guest's story and asking questions the audience wanted to ask. She won the respect of guests because she gave them respect and was genuinely interested in them. Guests knew that if they had been abused or unsuccessful with dieting, she understood. Soon, all Baltimore was talking about her, and the show ratings climbed. She said to herself, 'This is what I should be doing, it's like breathing.'[61]

"Of course, I'm talking about Oprah Winfrey. Oprah had found a career she had a passion for, one in which her apparent weakness—her ability to see from the viewpoint of others—was valuable human expertise.

"These days, *The Oprah Winfrey Show* is seen by twenty-million viewers per week. People invest hundreds of millions of dollars in the products she supports. Oprah used her leadership and business expertise to build a billion-dollar business. She has a lesson to teach all of us. When we learn to see from other's viewpoints, we show our respect for them and we gain their respect."

Marcus began to walk more briskly. As we rounded a corner where the outer portion of the road had fallen into the valley, we entered clouds. I slowed down to keep the edge of the road in sight. After ten minutes, watching every step and hearing only my breathing and the crunching under my shoes, I saw morning sunlight through the clouds above. I stopped as I cleared the top of the clouds. There was Marcus, his ankles in a mist, appearing to walk on the top of the clouds. It fit my image of him.

"Turn and look back," he said.

I turned. West of us, another mountain peak rose above the flat shelf formed by a soft, white cloud. Southwest of us, the shelf ended. The blue Mediterranean spread to the horizon.

"Beautiful," I said. "Did you know we'd climb above the clouds?"

He pointed down. "When we rounded that corner and the quarry appeared, you looked down. I looked up to see that where we are now standing was above the clouds. Visionaries know that there is great opportunity above because they see it from below. Or, having been to the top, they know that the journey is worth it. But others may see just a few steps ahead. I knew you would follow me, regardless. But it generally is a mistake to assume that others will follow. Great leaders know that others are more willing to follow when they 'see' what is at the top and find personal meaning in climbing to reach it."

The Customer's Point of View

"Intuit Corporation,[62] the maker of popular personal and small-business accounting software, continually searches for what existing customers 'see.' All Intuit employees, including the CEO, are required periodically to man the customer-service telephones and respond to and solve customers' problems. Customer thank-you letters are posted on the company's walls for all to see. At company meetings, the first items on the agenda are customer-service trends, problems, and victories. This tells the employees what the customers 'see' and what the employees are doing to please the customers.

"Seeing from the customer's point of view has created breakthrough marketing approaches. For example, dozens of patents were awarded for safety razors around the turn of the twentieth century.[63] Among them was one by King Gillette. His razor was different from, but not superior to, many of the others. It cost a dollar to produce his razor—more than he could sell one for. But Gillette figured out the shaver's point of view. The shaver would buy his razor if it were priced at fifty-five cents, well below the competitors' prices. After that, the shaver would willingly pay five cents each for the blades. As a blade cost less than a cent to make, Gillette could afford a big loss on the razor while making a profit on sales of blades. He made money on the shave, not on the razor."

I said, "Xerox did a similar thing by placing expensive copiers in offices and charging five cents per copy."

John Mariotti

"Mike, I know you've met John Mariotti and you know that in the late 80's he led Huffy Bicycle to a dominant position in the U.S. bicycle market. What you may not know is that one of the secrets to Huffy's success was their relentless search to discover their customer's point of view.

One year at their National Sales Meeting, at six in the morning, they set up floodlights outside their meeting hotel and aimed them at over one hundred boxes of bicycles. Half the boxes contained Huffy bicycles and half were imports. They then handed tool kits to their salespeople and

The teacher, if indeed wise, does not bid you to enter the house of his wisdom, but leads you to the threshold of your own mind.
Kahlil Gibran[64]

asked them to open, assemble, and ride a bike to breakfast—or failing that, to walk the 2 miles to breakfast! Stories of what they learned in that experience went on for years.

Each day their 2000 employees had to walk past a display of Huffy's product and competitor's with features and prices in the entrance to their factory lunchroom. They were encouraged to write down what they felt and post it at the display. One employee's comment was, "These bikes don't look cheap at all; they look so good that it's scary."

They would periodically order pizza into their bike showroom for their customer service group, product managers, engineers, and quality people. They would then open a few of their boxed bikes and a few of the competitors' and assemble them to see how well they went together. At every session, the people learned new things about their product—from the customer's perspective.

Each holiday season, Huffy's staff and occasionally a couple of Union officials would "go shopping" in areas where their top 5-6 customers had stores to see how their bikes matched up at the point where consumers 'voted with their money'. One year, a Union official asked, "Will they really pay that much more for our bikes?"

John and his team developed many other creative ways so they could see the bicycle buying and owning experience from their customers' eyes."

"Marcus, I know that after John left Huffy, he served as President of Rubbermaid Office Products Group. What is he doing today?"

"After Rubbermaid, John was sought after by many corporations as a management consultant and speaker. He has authored seven books and serves on the board of directors of several corporations. I just re-read his insightful book 'Marketing Express'. He is currently the CEO of the Enterprise Group. He's my candidate for filling Peter Drucker's shoes."

John believes that, 'Companies and businesses exist because someone had a need or want and someone else fulfilled that need with a product or service.' John asks four questions: 'How did that person know such a need existed? How did he or she develop a product or service that met that need? How did he or she communicate that such a product or service existed? How was the original person with a need convinced to buy that product, when there were many others that were similar and might have fulfilled the need?' John's answer is marketing, marketing, and marketing. Notice that the answer to all of John's questions is know-ing the customer's needs."

The Employee's Point of View

"Finding what it takes to energize employees to give more than what the job requires is an important leadership function. Employees may want more training or increased responsibility in their jobs. They may want to have a say in how the work is done. They may want to be part of a mission with a high purpose. They may want more job security. It is important to see the world from their points of view.

"We are climbing Mount Sagro, one of the highest peaks in the Alpi Apuanes," Marcus said, as we reached a plateau where wildflowers were blooming.

"Wild orchids?" I asked

"Yes, one must climb this high to see them."

For the last fifty yards, we scrambled through and over some rocks. At the top, Marcus opened his backpack, removed a small black blanket with a Roman army insignia on it, and spread it out. He sat on a rock beside it. From the backpack, he also removed a thermos bottle and two small cups. "Ah, cappuccino," he said.

"I thought you drank espresso," I commented.

"But you like cappuccino," he replied, pouring and handing me a cup.

"Thanks," I said. I was amused. Even on top of a mountain, Marcus had his coffee.

How Do We Find The High Meanings That Others Will Change For?

Marcus sipped his cappuccino, then said, "Great leaders search for the high meaning that will inspire others to give their minds and hearts."

"In nineteen forty," he continued, "personal survival was on every British citizen's mind. At that time, Great Britain stood alone in Europe against a mighty German war machine that had swept through Poland, Czechoslovakia, and France. It was clear that Hitler would soon attack the British homeland. As concerned British citizens huddled around the radio, the Prime Minister, Sir Winston Churchill, spoke in the clipped and inspiring tones he was famous for.[65]

Winston Churchill

'Hitler knows he will have to break us on this island or lose the war. If we can stand up to him, all Europe will be free, and the life of the world may move forward into broad, sunlit uplands. But if we fail, the whole world, including the United States, including all we have known and cared for, will sink into the abyss of a new Dark Age. . . . Let us therefore brace ourselves to our duties and so bear ourselves that if the British Empire and its commonwealth last for a thousand years, men will say, 'This was our finest hour.'"

"His speech roused the spirit of the people, elevating them above their fear, above their self-interest. In the darkest hour of the twentieth century, Churchill stood like a shining light. He knew what influenced human action.

"There are many theories about what influences our actions. Some of the most respected theories are:

- There are meanings programmed in us for survival and adaptation
- The culture we live in is a great influence on our adaptive behavior
- There is a hierarchy of human needs
- We all have a need for meaning

I'll begin with the most basic theory."

There are Meanings Programmed in Us for Survival and Adaptation

"Some anthropologists theorize that humans are programmed to survive and adapt by rewarding two opposite behaviors: caution and adventure," Marcus said. "It's as if we are pulled in two opposite directions. The adventurous pull rewards us for exploring, risk taking, discovering, pushing our limits, and fighting. The cautious pull rewards us when we rest our minds and bodies, conserve our energy and resources, preserve ourselves, and flee from danger. One opportunity may have very different meanings for different people. The cautious individual may see danger in the opportunity, while the adventurous individual sees excitement and rewards. Most leaders are on the adventurous side and they often are impatient with those on the cautious side. They prod others to explore, to take risks, to set unimaginable goals, to make changes."

"That's leadership," I said.

The Culture We Live in Is a Great Influence on Our Adaptive Behavior

Marcus nodded. "For example, the Chinese were the first to make paper, to make silk, to use block letters to print, to invent gunpowder, to create the first water-driven machine for the spinning of hemp, and to use coal and coke in blast furnaces. Although they found all these opportunities, the opportunities all were seized and turned into huge enterprises by the Europeans. David Landes,[66] a researcher, says that not only did the ancient Chinese lack free markets and property rights, they didn't seize these opportunities because they valued tradition, and the leaders wanted to keep the power in their hands. They were cautious, whereas the Europeans were adventuresome. The Chinese culture today is becoming more adventuresome. "

There Is a Hierarchy of Human Needs

"Another popular theory is the psychologist Abraham Maslow's hierarchy of needs,"[67] he said.

"According to Maslow, basic needs at the bottom of the hierarchy must be satisfied before higher needs become important. Maslow said that whatever needs a person is experiencing affect the person's motivations, priorities, and behaviors. Unsatisfied needs create the motivation to satisfy them. People need to satisfy the needs at each lower level—at least partially—before they can move on to a higher level."

"Many of the people in the developed countries today are not focusing on mere survival. So they can focus on creating new products and developing themselves. In the most advanced countries, each year, more work requires innovation, and those who can innovate are functioning higher on Maslow's pyramid. Leaders in advanced countries who help people move toward the top of the pyramid will get them to give more than what is required."

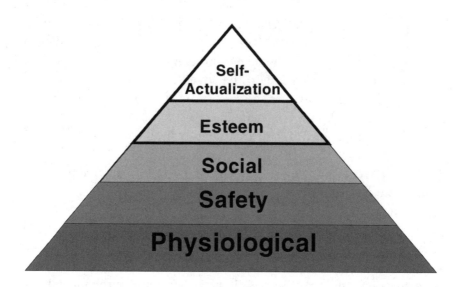

Maslow's Hierarchy of Needs

"Is self-actualization like finding one's personal David in the stone?" I asked

"Yes," he said. "Some behaviorists say that the higher the purpose, the higher the meaning. Why do you think people do volunteer work?"

"They believe in what they're doing," I answered.

"Is that all? What if they are asked to do work they don't enjoy doing?"

"For a good cause, a higher purpose, many would probably do it, although that wouldn't necessarily be the best use of their expertise. Others might resist." I said.

"So are you saying it is or it isn't enough for an organization to have a high purpose to get people to dedicate themselves toward its mission?"

"I studied the best volunteer organizations," I said. "They find what expertise a volunteer has and they look for a job in the organization where the person will be challenged to use his or her expertise to the fullest. Many volunteers I studied were more enthusiastic about their unpaid work than they were about what they did for a living."

"Yes!" he said. "The more freedom of choice and opportunities people have, the more we must work to find ways to get their willing contribution toward achievement of the mission. The most progressive of today's leaders treat all people they lead as if they're volunteers."

"As the amount of available knowledge increases rapidly, businesses must acquire knowledge more rapidly and more effectively in order to remain competitive. That means that the knowledge a worker has and his or her ability to use it are vital resources. Therefore, knowledgeable people have to be managed as if they were volunteers."

We All Have a Need for Meaning

Marcus continued, "Another theory that is relevant to our discussion is about man's need for meaning. Meanings are powerful beams of light in the worst darkness. In *Man's*

> *Man will put up with any "how" if he has a "why."*
> Nietzsche[68]

Search for Meaning,[69] Viktor Frankl, who survived German concentration camps, says that those who survived had meaning that made the brutal conditions tolerable. Some felt that they needed to take care of loved ones or that they still had unfinished work to do. Others felt that surviving was a way of winning over their hated captors. Frankl proposed that the highest meanings are those meanings for which people will endure any difficulty and choose to survive when death would be easier. He believed that meaning is the best motivator for development, improvement, and change."

"Mike, as I remember, in nineteen eighty-three, when competitors attacked, Jesse decided to move all of Dardenn's manufacturing to Singapore. But you changed his mind."

"I convinced him that we shouldn't move our production based simply on labor costs," I said. "That we should move some of our low-end products to countries like Japan and, later, China, where our products have local markets and we can compete. If you compete successfully with competitors in their own countries, they can't as easily raise the capital to mount attacks on you in your country. We're now the market-share leader for our products in Japan, and our business in China is growing rapidly. I also asked Jesse for a chance to reduce our manufacturing costs for the higher-cost models in the U.S.—enough to make them profitable again."

"You told me once that Jesse changed his mind when you asked him if he wanted to be remembered for putting hundreds of local people out of work."

"Yes! I can still remember the pained look on his face when I said that."

"Powerful! You found the higher meaning that influenced him."

"Jesse was a good man," I said. "He cared about the people. But his two boys don't."

"But you will influence them," he said.

"I don't know," I said.

Marcus stood and paced back and forth at the cliff's edge, looking down. Then he said, "The meaning something has is its significance, value, or importance to us. So the more we stand to lose by the absence of something or someone, the more meaning it or the person has for us."

The Meaning That Something or Someone Has for Us

- *The value, moral or psychological significance, need, or importance to us*
- *What we stand to lose by its or the person's absence*
- *What we stand to gain by acquiring it or having the person in our lives*

"In general," Marcus said, "no matter what theory of human behavior they were inclined to believe, the great leaders always searched for higher meanings when they were trying to influence others to change."

Marcus came back and sat down. He removed a neatly wrapped package from the backpack and unwrapped it. Inside were two pastries.

As I looked east, a range of mountains spread before us. "Beautiful," I said. I was grateful to be in the presence of wisdom and beauty. I stared at the pastries, thinking that I was at the bottom of Maslow's hierarchy of needs. Nevertheless, I wasn't going to be the first to reach for a pastry.

Converting People To Investors

"Our research team found that great leaders influenced others in a way we couldn't put into words," Marcus continued. "Traditional words, such as ownership, participation, and involvement, didn't describe how they led. Then one of our research staff leaders suggested that great leaders converted people into investors. Initially, no one agreed with her. She said that the team members were thinking too narrowly about the word 'investor.' She asked them to think of broader definitions of invest, such as 'devote time or provide ideas to a purpose' or 'contribute effort to something in the hope of future benefit.' For example, if someone on your staff willingly proposes a better way to do a job, she's an investor. However, if she thinks you won't listen to her, or that she'll lose if her idea fails, she may not invest. If one of your engineers willingly works unpaid over a weekend to test a new product, he's an investor. The time you willingly give your children is an investment. Our staff leader said that thinking of people as potential investors of their time, ideas, and resources greatly improves the ways in which we approach them for their help. In time, all of us agreed that converting people to investors was the best way to describe what great leaders did to mobilize people to seize opportunities."

"We decided that, from that point on, we would define an investor as 'any person or group that willingly gives time, ideas, or resources to seize an opportunity, in the hope of future benefit.'

> **Investor:** Any person or group that willingly gives time, ideas, or resources to seize an opportunity, in the hope of future benefit.

"So, to mobilize support, we should first identify those who should be involved and then learn what meanings influence their behaviors. We are then prepared to convert them to investors by taking the next three actions: co-creating with the eager ones, selling the cautious ones, and finding common meaning with the opposers. It's important to be skilled in all three actions. It's also important to know which action will be most effective with each group."

I looked at the pastries, thinking that I'd be willing to make an investment for one of them.

Willingness To Invest Time, Mind, and Resources

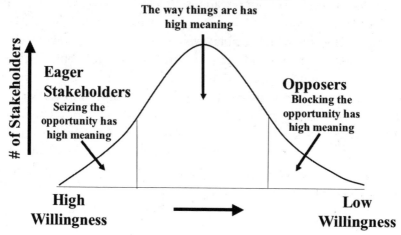

Willingness to Invest

"When an opportunity first is introduced, people's willingness to invest varies widely." Marcus pulled the manuscript out of the backpack, flipped over a few pages, and handed it to me, pointing as he did so. "In the drawing, people are divided into three groups, according to their willingness to invest and what has the most meaning for them."

"A small group of people, the 'eager stakeholders'—sometimes called 'early adopters' or 'pioneers'—are looking for opportunity and are willing to change. Seizing the opportunity has high meaning for them. A much larger group, the 'cautious stakeholders,' wants to keep things the way they are, because keeping things the way they are has high meaning for them. Many of them are pragmatic, however, and can be sold on the opportunity. Another small group, the 'opposers,' initially will oppose the opportunity, either because the individuals believe that the opportunity is against their interests or because they're championing other opportunities that compete for the same resources. Blocking the opportunity has high meaning for them."

Co-Create with Those Eager for Opportunity

People support what they create.

Kurt Lewin

Marcus said, "Great leaders have the answer to the question: How do we influence those who are most eager to invest? They are often those who eagerly seek opportunity, have high motivation for change, and will influence others."

6. Co-create with those eager for opportunity

- How do we influence those who are most willing to invest? , those who eagerly seek opportunity, those who have high motivation for change, those who will influence others?

How Do We Influence Those Who Are Most Eager To Invest?

"My next great innovator's ability to influence those most eager to invest was critical to his seizing a great opportunity. Let me begin his story at the moment he faced bankruptcy."

Co-creation

"After months of preparation, in early nineteen seventy-three, Fred Smith, his wife, and his office staff stood at the end of a runway on a small airfield in Memphis. They were waiting for six small jets to arrive with packages to be delivered overnight. A makeshift conveyor and sorting table were set up in an old hangar, and employees were standing by. Everyone knew that this was the last chance. All day, reports from sales agents had been optimistic, and Fred was ready to celebrate. Just before midnight, six tiny lights appeared in the sky. After the jets landed and roared to a stop, everyone moved toward them. When the doors of the first plane were opened, the group looked into the cargo hold to see the contents."

"Empty! They looked into the other planes; there were only five paid packages. The group couldn't believe it. Fred was shocked. Surely now, his family, financial backers, friends, and staff believed, Fred would come to his senses, give up overnight package delivery, and do something else for a living. Three strikes and you're out."

"Fred's first two strikes were also in the overnight delivery business. He first attempted to deliver securities overnight for bond houses. But, when insurers wouldn't financially guarantee the shipments, his business fizzled. Second, he decided to fly checks between Federal Reserve Banks. The Feds encouraged him because they could envision big savings. But by the time Fred bought two airplanes, named his company Federal Express, and was ready with a working system, the Feds had scrapped the idea."

"Then Fred came up with the idea of overnight package delivery. His company would pick up packages, fly them to Memphis and sort them, then deliver them to their destinations the next morning. Fred chose six cities close to Memphis for his trial run. He bought four more planes, expanded his crew, and hired a sales force. The result was the six planes with only the five paid packages that I just talked about."

"On the edge of bankruptcy, Fred asked his team members to stick with the business and to invest their time to help him create a successful overnight delivery business. They agreed. After two weeks of sixteen-hour-a-day analysis, the team members decided they had chosen the wrong cities to start with. They had chosen cities a short flight from Memphis rather than cities that needed the service. For example, they'd picked New Orleans, which had a weak industrial base and was serviced well by Delta Airlines. So they searched for cities that had strong industries and weren't serviced well, like Rochester, New York, the home of Kodak and Xerox—cities that most needed overnight delivery."

"In April, Fred and his team gathered again at midnight at the airport, waiting for the planes to return from the newly selected destinations. They all agreed that they had given it their best shot. If it didn't work this time, they were through. After the planes rolled to a stop, the group quietly approached. When the first plane's cargo doors were opened, they again pressed to look into the hold. They were surprised and elated; the planes were filled with hundreds of packages. The team's plan had worked, and they now were committed for better or worse."

"Shortly afterward, it did get worse. In one crisis, while juggling his cash to keep the company afloat, Fred issued a memo with all employees' paychecks, stating that they were welcomed to cash their checks, but that it would be helpful if some of them waited a few days. Almost everyone waited. Some employees never cashed those checks. Many of them proudly have the framed checks hanging on their office walls."

"Fred's team continued to fight its way through obstacles until FedEx was delivering thousands of packages each day. It was the fastest company in history to reach one billion dollars in sales. Today, FedEx delivers two-and-a-half million packages per night and is a twenty-four-billion-dollar enterprise."[70]

"Great leaders like Fred know how to influence those who are eager for opportunity, those who are often called 'early adopters.' When those eager for opportunity are willing to invest, they'll influence others to invest. In the drawing, there is a dark area on the left side that represents this group." Marcus showed me the drawing in his manuscript.

"Effective leaders, like Fred, work with those who are eager for opportunity to jointly create the opportunity, so they are willing to invest in seizing it. I call this co-creation. Co-creation works because, as Kurt Lewin said, 'people support what they create', and everyone has

Willingness To Invest Time, Mind, and Resources

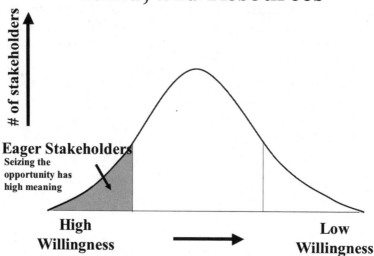

# of stakeholders

Eager Stakeholders
Seizing the
opportunity has
high meaning

**High
Willingness**

**Low
Willingness**

something creative to contribute. *This is the first law of meaning: People support what they create."*

First Law of Meaning: People Support What They Create. "Co-creation is a timeless action. In A.D. one hundred, Columella, a Roman landlord, wrote about managing his workforce: 'Nowadays, I make it a practice to call them into consultation on any new work. I observe they're more willing to set about a piece of work when their opinions are asked and their advice followed.'"

"Edison co-created with his team. A machinist who worked for Edison for fifty years said, 'He made

> *First Law of Meaning: People Support What They Create.*

me feel I was making something with him; not just a workman.'"

"By building environments that favor co-creation, organizations increase their chances that eager investors will step forward and invest their time and ideas. For example, in the late nineteen eighties, NASA asked Lockheed Martin to cut the weight of the huge fuel tank that forms the backbone of the space shuttle. An engineering team used stronger, lighter-weight materials to reduce the weight, but fell eight hundred pounds short of the target. However, Lockheed Martin had widely dispersed the knowledge of the target to the workforce. One line worker knew that two hundred gallons of paint was being used to paint the tank and he knew that a gallon weighed about four pounds, amounting to

> **Co-creating:** Creating an opportunity with others in such a way that they willingly invest in seizing it.

a total weight of eight hundred pounds. He also knew the tank had a ten-minute life span before it was jettisoned. He suggested that they stop painting the tank. The engineers listened, and NASA agreed. The line worker invested his idea because management was open to co-creation."

"Mike," Marcus asked, "after you talked Jesse out of moving all of Dardenn's manufacturing operations overseas, how did you convince people to make enough improvements to become competitive?"

"I explained the situation to the members of our workforce and asked for their help," I said. "We formed cost-reduction teams and set a goal of fourteen-percent cost reduction by year's end. You had showed us how to find great improvement opportunities. We found them and seized them."

"When you asked for their help you showed respect for their expertise," Marcus said. "Few leaders have more respect for the expertise of others than Norman Bodek. He is the founder of Productivity Inc., and is the acknowledged founding father of the Lean movement in this country. In the early eighties he introduced American business to the very productive methods of Japanese manufacturers. Norm believes that every person has the capacity and desire to be a problem solver and to be a source of creative ideas. Norm's mission was once suggested in a Chinese fortune

Norman Bodek

cookie he read. It said, 'You have the talent to recognize the talent in others'. With many great successes to his credit, Norm now spends his time teaching managers how to help people use their creative abilities. He founded the publishing company, PCS Press, to spread his message. 'I see myself,' he says, 'as the Johnny Appleseed of empowering people to believe in themselves and their creative abilities'. He is a much sought after speaker and consultant."

Marcus handed me one of the pastries. I put the manuscript down and ate the pastry slowly, hoping to convince my stomach that it was a three-course meal. We sat quietly in the sun's warmth.

After about five minutes, Marcus stirred. "Let's continue to the next action of the great ones," he said. "Even adventuresome people have difficulty changing what's been good to them for many years. Even when logic says 'change or else' or when the situation is highly uncomfortable, they may hold on to the way things are. Why do you suppose that is?"

"Either they have a lot invested in the way things are or they've experienced too much change lately. Or, maybe, they don't mind change but they mind being changed."

His eyes widened. "Good point," he said. "Most people are not easily changed; they are cautious and pragmatic. Let's examine why they're cautious."

Sell Opportunity to Those
That Are Cautious

*You must change people's minds. And you can't just root out a
handful of complex ideas and leave a void behind—you have to
give people something that is as meaningful as what they've lost!*
Daniel Quinn[71]

"**O**ver the years," Marcus said, "the medical field has been
cautious—for good reasons. However, one of the most important medical breakthroughs in history was made because
an eager surgeon was influenced by a great scientist to seize an opportunity. At the time, doctors ridiculed a new idea that tiny germs could
kill a large animal or a human. They believed that germs spontaneously
appeared and that people either inherited their susceptibility to them
or succumbed because they were being punished for evildoing. Then a
French scientist, Louis Pasteur, discovered that germs could kill large
animals and that germs came from
other diseased persons or animals.
However, as late as eighteen seventy-two, a professor at Toulouse
said that Pasteur's germ theory
was ridiculous fiction. Pasteur in-
furiated doctors by saying that
fifty percent of all surgery patients
died because they were infected
during surgery. He proposed that
surgeons disinfect themselves,
their instruments, and the area of
the patient that was open during
surgery. Influenced by Pasteur's
writings, a surgeon named Joseph

Louis Pasteur

Lister developed antiseptic methods that reduced the death rate from his surgeries from nearly fifty percent to twelve percent. Others followed Lister. In the next ten years, thousands of surgeons adopted his methods."

"Almost all major innovations in history were spread only after some eager investor produced results so impressive that some of the cautious ones were willing to try the idea."

The Concerns Of The Cautious

"People are cautious for good reasons. Their caution often is expressed in the personal and business questions they ask when they are asked to make changes. The personal questions are:

- Why should we change? Why now? Why us? Why me?
- What if I make a mistake? Will I be worse off after the change?
- What will my new job be? What will the new organization look like?
- How and when will the change be made?
- Does the organization care about what happens to me?
- Will I have a say in what happens, or will they ignore what I think?
- Will I have a role or position as good as the one I have today?
- Will my expertise be as needed and as valuable?
- Will I lose power or influence? Whom will I work for? Will I have a job at all?
- If I lose my job, how will I support my family?
- Where will I find another job?"

"The Business questions and considerations are:
- Is the technology proven?
- Is this opportunity for real and long term or is it just another wild idea or passing fad?
- Is there a clear, low-risk return on any investment we might make?
- Who else in my market has done this? Were they successful?
- We already have our plates full; where would we get the resources?
- Why can't we wait until the opportunity is more widely tried and proven successful?

- Will my boss or the rest of the organization buy into it?
- What is the hidden downside to the perceived opportunity?
- Is there a safe exit strategy if it doesn't work?"

"The researcher Everett Rogers[72] found five factors that determine how fast innovations are adopted within a culture:

- The relative advantage that the new method or technology has
- How compatible it is with adopters' existing beliefs and customs
- How simple and easy it is to use
- How easily it can be tried or experienced
- How observable the results are"

Notice that all five factors are viewed from the eyes of the potential adopter.

"A large number of cautious people want to keep things the way they are—not only because the way things are has high meaning for them but also because they would rather wait until the opportunity has been proved before they invest. I show this in another drawing in the manuscript." Marcus leafed through several pages and pointed to a drawing.

Willingness To Invest Time, Mind, and Resources

Cautious Stakeholders

The way things are has high meaning

# of Stakeholders

High Willingness

Low Willingness

7. Sell the opportunity to those that are cautious

- How do we influence stakeholders who have high meaning in their present state? , who are skeptical, who don't like change, or who are change weary?

"To get this large group to invest, we must be able to answer the question: How do we influence those who have high meaning with their present states?, who are skeptical, who don't like change, or who are change weary?

How Do We Influence Those Who Are Skeptical, Pragmatic, Or Resistant To Change?

"High achievers have high meaning with the present state and often are the most cautious of all the stakeholders."

Influencing the High Achievers

"As I said before, those who found an area of work in which they had high expertise, high passion, and would be well rewarded often found and seized great opportunities that made them highly successful. So when they see that the new opportunity is in a field or area of work where they have less expertise, or where they have less passion, or where the rewards may be less, they may be cautious about change. Let me give you an example that shook a company and its people to their foundations."

"In the late nineteen eighties, Motorola was the dominant player in the mobile-phone business, with a world market share of thirty-five percent. In the nineteen nineties, Nokia, an upstart in the mobile-phone business, offered phones with digital technology, and digital technology became the European standard. As Nokia's market share grew steadily, Motorola was cautious and resisted moving into the digital phone business. In fact, Motorola increased its investment and effort in analog mobile phones. By the end of the year two thousand, Nokia's world market share increased to thirty-five percent while Motorola's dropped to fifteen percent. Does it sound strange that Motorola saw the rewards shifting to digital mobile-phone makers, yet resisted moving in that direction? This is another paradox."

The Differentiation Paradox

"Differentiating ourselves for opportunity is essential to finding great opportunity. Yet that same differentiation can keep us from finding opportunities in a market or an industry that has changed greatly. For example, a small retailer may be faced with a Wal-Mart down the street that offers the same products at thirty-percent less. A wholesale distribution business may be faced with a major retailer, such as Wal-Mart, that is buying directly from factories in China. A manager in a manufacturing plant must learn lean manufacturing methods or lose business to a manufacturer in Korea. When world markets change rapidly, the way in which we have differentiated our business for opportunity, the work for which we have high expertise and high passion, may no longer be well rewarded."

"So we have a paradox: the way we differentiated ourselves was the key to our success, but now it keeps us from finding and seizing opportunities in the new marketplace. Unless we can change the way in which we are differentiated, we will lose the rewards. But how could we have convinced engineers that were experts in analog mobile-phone technology that they should learn digital phone technology? People must not only see that they must differentiate themselves in a new way, they must also see that they can become experts in the new technology and they must see a clear path to doing that."

Influencing Those Who Have Achieved Less in the Past

"Those who have achieved less in the past often are cautious because their past experiences with change have not been good or because they are change-weary. They may have found areas of work in which they are moderately successful and, although they may not be totally pleased with their situations, they have settled for their places in life. They often resist change."

"It's as if there's a law of human inertia that applies to both high and low achievers," Marcus said. "Let me use a physics analogy."

> *We have been disappointed before, swindled by promises that it seemed—and were—too good to be true. . . . Our worries are our safe boundaries; over time we have learned to identify with our limits. Now, leery of trusting the promise of an oasis, we defend the merits of the desert.*
> Marilyn Ferguson[73]

Meaning and the Physics of Change

"Galileo discovered a remarkable fact about motion: A body in motion will continue to move at the same speed in the same direction forever if it's not acted on by an inside or outside force. This is called Galileo's Law of Inertia or Newton's First Law.[74]

"If we could extend Newton's Laws to changes in humans and businesses, we might propose a Second Law of Meaning. This law would say that many individuals and organizations will continue in the same direction, at the same speed, unless they are acted on by an inside or outside force."

"It's as if there's a law of meaning that says that the more meaning humans have invested in the way things are, the more they'll resist efforts to seize new opportunities that change the way things are."

> *Second Law of Meaning: Many Individuals and Organizations Will Continue in Their Same Directions, at the Same Speeds, Unless They Have Higher Meaning to Change Their Directions or Speeds.*

Inertia and Meaning

"Some leaders assume that cautious people will be willing if they see the benefits of an opportunity," Marcus said. "They're frustrated when others are skeptical and reluctant to change."

I said, "Since 'the way things are' has high meaning for cautious people, they often resist change until they're in trouble. That's why the biggest need for progress and the largest opportunities usually are in organizations that cautious people are managing. To get them to change, there must be dissatisfaction with the way things are or an urgent, compelling case for change, or a higher meaning."

"That's true," he said. "We must help the cautious to see that, if they don't find and seize the opportunities, others will pass them by, and they will lose what they have. The best leaders also help them to find higher meaning in the new opportunity."

Help the Cautious Find Higher Meaning in a Mission

"Steve Jobs has an extraordinary ability to get others to invest in a dream—to convert them into investors. He converted the Macintosh computer-development team by promising that it would 'put a dent in the universe.'"

"So did Edison," I added. "One of his assistants said that Edison told them they were not inventing an electric light, they were dispelling night with its darkness . . . from the arena of civilization."

Marcus nodded. "At Gettysburg, after a battle that caused nearly fifty thousand casualties, President Lincoln appealed to the highest meanings when he said, 'that from these honored dead we take increased devotion to that cause for which they gave the last full measure of devotion—that we here highly resolve that these dead shall not have died in vain—that this nation, under God, shall have a new birth of freedom—and the government of the people, by the people, for the people, shall not perish from the earth.'"

"These leaders converted cautious people by helping them to find the highest meanings in their missions and then helping them to find great opportunities to accomplish their missions."

"Mike, you know the old story about the philosopher and the happy stone mason that I have in the journal?"

I said that I did.

The Happy Stonemason

Once upon a time, an ancient philosopher passed three stonemasons and asked each of them what they were doing. The first, an obviously unhappy man, dismissed the philosopher in a gruff tone, saying that he was just doing his job. The second was pleasant and polite in his response, showing and explaining to the philosopher how an artist carves a stone. But when the philosopher asked the third, an exuberantly happy man, what he was doing, the third man beamed and said, "I'm building a cathedral."

"The great leader knows that shaping a stone has higher meaning when the stone is part of a cathedral. So he or she helps cautious people to see the cathedral they will be building. Louise Francesconi, vice president of Raytheon's Missile Division, believes that the reward people get is seeing the vision and result as theirs. She believes that people like to go to work when they feel that what they do is important and when they feel that they are the best in the world at what they do—when they feel they are the best missile-makers in the world."[75]

"Rather than keeping them in the dark," I said. "Or expecting them to do the job just because they're paid."

Actively Search for Higher Meaning with Cautious People

"How do you find high meanings that people at Dardenn will invest in?" he asked me.

"I ask them questions, such as, 'What do you feel is the most important issue facing you or our business?' and 'What are the most important opportunities or threats for us in the future?' and 'What concerns you most right now?' I try to imagine how I would think and feel in their situations. I look for changes they'll support. I ask, 'If you could have any wish you wanted, what would you wish for?' and 'What would you change if you could change anything you want?' During the questioning, I regularly feed back to them what I think they said, to make sure I got the meanings right. Finally, I ask questions based on guesses I make about what they'll willingly support."

"Good questions and a good approach," Marcus said. "In the manuscript, I have some recommendations for searching for meaning. The first recommendation is to ask questions such as those you ask the people at Dardenn."

I flipped through the pages until I found them and then read the list.

Recommendations for Searching for Meaning

- *Ask questions aimed at uncovering another's point of view, goals, thoughts, feelings, fears, joys, hopes, wishes, understandings, values, beliefs, and/or highest meanings.*
- *Acknowledge that you heard by restating what you believe the person said.*
- *Clarify and validate the person's viewpoint.*
- *Avoid analysis, judgment, coloration, amplification, diminishing, evaluation, or disagreement with the person's point of view.*
- *Carefully probe deeper when you find something that means a lot to the person.*
- *Acknowledge that you understand and respect what means a lot to him or her.*
- *Search for a benefit from the opportunity that will have high meaning for the person.*
- *If possible, redesign the opportunity so that it has high meaning for all who have a stake in it.*

"Finding out what means a lot to people is easier said than done," I said.

"None of this is easy," he replied. "What I'm saying is that it's worth it. Suppose you could influence Ron Dardenn to care more about the people at Dardenn?"

"I have little influence on Ron."

Marcus frowned. "You don't?" he asked, surprised.

"Jesse made me president in the last months of his life. But, in Jesse's will, he left each of the boys thirty-three percent of the company stock, so they can do whatever they want. Ron has expertise in sales and marketing, but neither one of them has the expertise to run a company.

"They'll realize quickly how much they need you," he said.

"You don't know them. They think they already know everything."

"Mike, why is it that sometimes those who need expertise the most don't think they need it?"

I tried to steer the conversation away from the problems at Dardenn. I not only wanted to hear the rest of the findings on selling opportunity to the cautious, I was now very interested in what they had learned about dealing with opposers. "From what you said earlier, when we ask people to give up meaning, we should co-create a replacement meaning," I replied.

"Yes," he agreed, "the best leaders also help the cautious people find meaning in every step of the finding-and-seizing process. They don't find opportunity for others; they help them to find it. They don't design or plan the opportunity for others; they help them to find opportunity that has high meaning for them. They don't implement for others; they support them and remove barriers as they implement. They don't provide the high meaning for others; they help them to find it. As Lao-Tzu said two thousand five hundred years ago: 'Of a good leader, when his work is done, his aim fulfilled, they will all say, we did this ourselves.'"

"Once they have helped the cautious see how they must change to seize the new opportunities, they help them to see a pathway to developing the new expertise and, sometimes, they help them to find the passion they need to seize the new opportunities. The best leaders lead by example. In the early nineteen eighties, Andy Grove, the CEO of Intel, saw that Intel could no longer make profits in the computer-memory business. He decided to move the company to become a producer of microprocessors. As soon as he made the decision, Andy spent a large portion of his time personally learning about microprocessors and how they make software work in computers. He asked his internal people and outside software people to help him learn the new expertise. He told his executive staff that half of them had better become software experts in five years' time. In other words, Grove set the example by changing his expertise and his passion. By nineteen eighty-five, as microprocessor sales grew, Intel had closed eight memory plants and left the memory business. By nineteen ninety-six, it had over eighty percent of the world's microprocessor business, over twenty billion dollars in sales, and twice the profit rate it had in nineteen eighty-five. Now, Intel's name is synonymous with microprocessors.

"Finally, before they begin the seizing process, great leaders find common meaning and negotiate with those who will oppose any seizing of the opportunity."

Find Common Meaning with and Negotiate with Opposers

Most people hate resistance. Because it is viewed so negatively, people want to get over it. In the words of many articles on the subject, people want to overcome resistance. This view is wrong. Attempts to overcome it usually make it worse.

Rick Maurer[76]

"**G**reat leaders know that opposers are simply protecting what has meaning to them or are champions of other opportunities that are competing for the same resources. So they study what the other opportunities offer and they search for ways to either convert the opposers or reduce their negative effects. However, like Galileo, leaders sometimes take the worst approach with those who oppose them."

"The question is: What's the best way to convert or reduce the negative effects of those who want to stop us from seizing opportunity?"

What's The Best Way To Convert Or Reduce The Negative Effects Of Those Who Want To Stop Us From Seizing Opportunity?

"There are three ways in which the great innovators and achievers converted or reduced the negative effects of those who wanted to stop them from seizing opportunities. These are:
- Include opposing viewpoints
- Find common meaning
- Use force only as a last resort"

8. Find common meaning with and negotiate with opposers

- What's the best way to convert or reduce the negative effects of those who want to stop us from seizing opportunity?

Include Opposing Viewpoints

"Mike, in its short history, the United States has faced several crises that have threatened its existence. In each crisis, a leader emerged who was able to bring together opposing sides to seize the opportunity to survive. One crisis took place in late nineteen sixty-two. U.S. spy planes flying over Cuba took pictures showing that the Cubans were building a nuclear missile site that could reach most U.S. cities. President John F. Kennedy put a team together to analyze the situation and recommend action. By the end of the first day, it was nearly unanimous that the U.S. should launch a surprise air-attack, followed by an invasion. But Kennedy knew that Russian soldiers at the missile sites would be killed by air strikes, which would escalate the situation to a U.S.-Russian conflict. He and his brother, Robert ('Bobby'), remembered a disastrous decision they had made eighteen months earlier, when they decided to secretly help a band of Cuban exiles invade Cuba at the Bay of Pigs. The CIA had predicted that people in Cuba would join the invading force and then rise up and overthrow Castro. The invasion was a disaster. The Cuban military captured and humiliated the invaders by parading them through the streets of Havana. When President Kennedy appointed a blue-ribbon committee to decide what went wrong, the committee members said that the President was to blame because he decided on an answer before weighing alternatives. They said that his brother, Bobby, had shut off all cabinet opposition to the invasion. The brothers were so shook by the report, they changed their fundamental approach to decision making, never again deciding on an answer until all the options had been developed and all opposers' viewpoints had been considered.

"So, during the missile crisis, Bobby Kennedy asked the team to come up with other responses. On the third day of struggling for options, someone suggested a limited blockade as a first step. Some members of the group thought that a limited blockade would open a window for negotiation. Others saw it as a first step toward an air strike, an ultimatum. Eventually, the whole group agreed on a limited blockade as a first step.

"The next day, President Kennedy presented the plan to the Joint Chiefs of Staff, saying that the blockade would serve as an ultimatum, followed by air strikes if needed. He talked to congressional leaders and then went on worldwide television and radio to announce a shipping quarantine of Cuba. He said that ships entering the quarantine zone would be stopped and searched. He warned that, if any missiles were fired from Cuba, the U.S. would launch a nuclear strike against the Soviets."

"In the next few days, we all held our breaths as Soviet ships headed toward the blockade. At the last minute, Premier Krushchev turned the ships and offered to remove the missiles in return for a U.S. promise not to invade Cuba. When one of Kennedy's team heard that the ships had turned, he said, 'We've just had a showdown, and the other guy blinked.'

"Recently declassified Soviet and U.S. documents indicate that the situation was more dangerous than the Kennedys imagined. Secret memos from Krushchev show that he was worried that he couldn't control Soviet officers in Cuba. The CIA estimated Soviet troop strength in Cuba at only a few thousand lightly armed men. Soviet documents reveal that there were forty thousand Soviet troops in Cuba at the time, equipped with battlefield nuclear weapons. An air strike or invasion could have triggered Armageddon."

"The Kennedys learned the importance of listening to opposing views and negotiating for solutions that took advantage of the collective wisdom of their advisors."

Find Common Meaning with Opposers

Marcus picked up the manuscript again and turned several pages before handing it to me. "As that drawing illustrates, opposers have a low willingness to invest in an opportunity. In fact, they will eagerly invest their time and resources to stop anyone from seizing the opportunity. Stopping the opportunity has high meaning to them."

The Kennedys used powerful negotiation techniques to bring opposing sides together. A few minutes ago, I gave you some recommendations for searching for meaning. The same recommendations apply to negotiating with opposers, with the addition of the following:

- Assume that opposers have legitimate reasons for their positions and their interests.
- Find the minimum terms that each opposer will accept.
- Find a common need or want.
- Negotiate a win-win plan if you can.

Willingness To Invest Time, Mind, and Resources

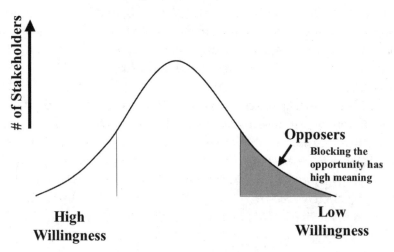

- Think of alternatives if you can't get a settlement. What will you do if either side refuses to budge, walks away, or escalates its opposition? Is time on your side or against you?"

"Marcus, if there ever was a time I needed to understand and apply these recommendations, it's now."

"Do you want to talk about it?"

I nodded and then explained the situation at Dardenn. Marcus asked many questions. I told him that I wasn't looking for an immediate answer but that I would appreciate it if he would think about it as we continued.

He said that he would and then he did continue. "Stephen Covey[81] says that win-win leaders see life more as a cooperative—not a competitive—arena, and that win-win thinking 'is based on a belief that there is plenty for everybody, that one person's success is not achieved at the expense or exclusion of the success of others.'"

Adversarial Negotiating

"There are those who feel that win-win thinking is weak-minded; that winning is the only thing; They believe the best negotiators are those who can negotiate the lion's share. They view negotiation as a contest where the best party wins at the others expense. The tactics of the win-lose negotiator are to negotiate from a position of strength, to set their demands so high initially that the final negotiated settlement is biased in their favor, and to act as if time is on their side. For nearly 100 years, beginning with violent strikes against the auto companies and recent strikes in American sports, union-management contract negotiations have been plaqued by adversarial negotiating. These are usually costly to all stakeholders. Many have led to permanent loss of jobs, the termination of unions, company bankruptcies, and loss of customers. In other words, there is a high risk that adversarial negotiation will end in lose-lose."

"It seems as if negotiation is just another form of co-creation," I said.

"You could think of it that way," he agreed.

"A leader can't always take the time to negotiate with the opposition," I continued. Sometimes you have to act in people's best interests, even when they don't agree."

"Like Ron Dardenn did?" he asked.

"He doesn't know what's best for the people."

"He thinks he does."

"Good point," I said. "The Dardenn boys believe that every opportunity creates winners and losers. Ron says that you can't make an omelet without cracking a few eggs. A few months ago, he fired two salesmen who disagreed with him. That sends a message. He doesn't negotiate with the opposition. Now everyone's willing to do whatever it takes to keep his or her job."

Marcus had a thoughtful look. "You bring up a good point. However, fear won't convert someone to become a willing investor, especially if he or she has other opportunities. People in fear may do what it takes to survive but, instead of devoting their creativity to seizing the opportunity, they may devote it to quietly sabotaging it. Even worse, creative people will leave organizations that dictate what they do. The best leaders design the opportunity with all involved so that everyone gains from seizing it," he said. "That's win-win thinking."

He reached over and turned a few more pages in the manuscript. "As I show in the drawing, over a period of time, an organization that takes the four actions to mobilize people's support increases its number of eager investors and their overall willingness to change. At the same time, it decreases the number of people in the organization who are opposed to change. Over time, as the organization increases its number of eager investors, it sees the opportunities in the changing world and creates its own future. The organization that fears and opposes change will have its future created for it."

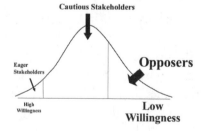

Organization That Doesn't Take the Four Multiplying Actions

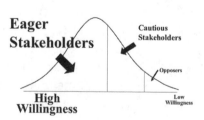

Organization That Takes the Four Multiplying Actions

Extreme Opposers

"In extreme cases, opposers will put you in prison or kill you if you seize the opportunity they oppose. In such cases, it takes great heroism to begin the seizing process. Occasionally a hero will rise, risk all, and plant seeds for change that profoundly alter the course of history. One great hero arose in China in nineteen seventy-eight. That year, farmers in the Chinese village of Xiaogang were starving. Chinese law forced them to turn their crops over to the government in exchange for such small amounts of grain that they could not feed their families. Witnessing the starvation, Yan Hongchang, the village leader, decided that death by starvation was so terrible, any punishment the government would inflict for violating the law could not be worse. He persuaded eighteen farmers to sign a pact that divided their land into family plots. They promised to turn their production quotas in to be given to the government but they would keep whatever remained—a violation of Chinese law. The agreement also said: 'In the case of failure, we are prepared for death or prison, and other commune members vow to raise our children until they are eighteen years old.'

"In nineteen seventy-nine, the leader of the commune of ten thousand members, which included Yan's village, accused the village of 'digging up the cornerstone of the revolution.' In desperation, Yan went to Chen, his county's Party secretary and a man with a reputation for having an open mind, and begged for help. Chen had heard that the group's harvests were good, so he agreed to protect the village so long as the practice didn't spread. Eventually, however, word of the violation made its way to Beijing and to China's new premier, Deng Xiaoping. The villagers braced for the worst.

"Deng surprised everyone. Instead of meting out punishment, he was so impressed with what the villagers had accomplished that he applauded them and directed that they be used as an example of what the Chinese farmer could do.

"Years later when Deng reflected on the rise of the village entrepreneurs, he was especially candid. He said, 'It was if a strange army appeared in the countryside, making and selling a huge variety of products. This is not the achievement of our central government. . . . This was not something I figured out. . . . This was a surprise.'

"The new philosophy of pragmatism that Deng sanctioned—believing that a method is good if it produces good economic results—

has spread throughout China and is fueling the largest industrial revolution in history.

"So if the opposers can destroy your life, it helps to seize an opportunity that is also a 'win' for them. It also helps to have a temporary protector to shield you until the rewards are delivered."

Use Force Only As a Last Resort

"When leaders become frustrated with opposition, they may react with force." He raised his hand with has palm open to me and pushed it suddenly toward me. "The problem is the word force! Rick Maurer,[78] a change consultant, says that when people react to resistance by using power, manipulating those who oppose, applying force of reason, ignoring resistance, playing off relationships, making deals, and killing the messenger, they lose effectiveness. Do you see a common thread in these reactions?"

He answered his own question. "They're all intended to overcome resistance. These reactions don't sell the opportunity to cautious investors, nor do these reactions help us to find common meaning and negotiate with opposers."

"This leads to a Third Law of Meaning that applies to opposers."

Third Law of Meaning: The More We Force Opposers to Give up What Has High Meaning to Them, the More They May Resist. "Leaders are at their best when they're co-creating, selling, and finding common meaning. They search for meanings that the opportunity can have for all who have a stake in it. They encourage people to express their needs, hopes, aspirations, concerns, and fears. They relax in the face of opposing views, letting others know that it is okay to express opposition."

> *Third Law of Meaning: The More We Force Opposers to Give up What Has High Meaning to Them, the More They May Resist.*

"Mike, do you have negative feelings when your views are questioned or attacked? When your motives or intentions are denounced? When others don't trust you? When they say they can't or won't do what's asked of them? When they say it can't be done? When they try to sabotage the effort you are leading?"

"Of course," I said.

During this conversation, Marcus capped the thermos bottle, picked up the blanket, folded it and put it in the backpack, and began to walk rapidly down the narrow road. I followed, still holding the manuscript. "You must have negative feelings towards Ron," he said. "Can you get past these feelings to find an opportunity in all this?"

I said, "I'm trying not to think about it while I'm reviewing your research." I smiled. "I'm still wondering if even you can find an opportunity in this mess."

"I'll do what I can," he said.

"Thanks, but let's finish discussing the actions you identified first," I said.

He nodded. We descended below the clouds. I kept up with him for a while, reminding myself as I rounded each blind corner that a road was there when we came up. Finally, I shouted, "I'd like to update my notes. See you at the bottom."

"Okay," he called back.

I could hear the crystals crunch under his boots for a few minutes, and then there was silence. I made some notes on the manuscript concerning the application of the recommendations to the Dardenn situation and resumed a fast walk. When I reached the car, Marcus was relaxing with an espresso. The driver offered me one. I thanked him and declined.

In the car, Marcus sat sideways in the front, looking back at me as he spoke. My attention was torn between the beautiful scenery, the drop-off at the edge of the road, and the tires squealing around corners. Marcus seemed unfazed by our racing descent.

Summary Of Actions To Mobilize Support

"In summary," he said, "great leaders search for the highest meanings of those who have a stake in the opportunity. They co-create the opportunity with them so that it produces the largest rewards they can get for their investment. They negotiate with opposers to minimize their resistance. In other words, they help all stakeholders to find and seize the highest-leverage, highest-meaning opportunities. That's what I help organizations to do."

"Search, find, and seize," I said. "It has a nice ring to it."

Santa Croce

At the outskirts of Florence, Marcus said something to our driver. After ten minutes of driving that would frighten a Shanghai cabbie, we pulled up in front of the Church of Santa Croce. Marcus motioned for me to follow him up the steps and into the church. It was dark in the church, with the only light falling from stained glass windows. Marcus pointed to a monument in the church wall. In a hushed voice he said, "Galileo is buried in there, with his daughter, Sister Maria Celeste."

Just to the right of Galileo's tomb, he stopped at a monument to Enrico Fermi, the physicist who conducted the first sustained nuclear reaction. He pointed to the plaque, "nineteen one to nineteen fifty-four: the dash between the dates—that's his life." He swept his hand across the church. "Musicians, philosophers, scientists, poets, and statesmen. Tonight, we'll discuss why they were chosen to lead again and again." We walked again, passing the tomb of Rossini. The floor and the walls were covered with flat, carved headstones. We stopped in front of Machiavelli's tomb.

I said, "Machiavelli believed that a leader should do whatever it takes to hold power." "Machiavelli didn't write about leadership; he wrote about ruling from a power position," Marcus said. "You should lead with the power of your mind even when you have position power."

"I have a hard time influencing the Dardenn boys," I said.

His eyebrows furrowed. "Do you think of them as boys?"

"Are you saying that I don't respect them?"

He stared at me. "Do they think you respect them?"

"I get your point.

We walked to the right, to the tomb of Michelangelo. "The works of Michelangelo live on," Marcus said. "It's important that the work that you and Jesse did live on."

"A lot of people depend on it," I said.

It was dark when we left the church. At the car, Marcus told me where to meet him for dinner. He said that the driver would drop me off at the apartment. Then he walked away. I turned my cell phone on.

Crisis At Dardenn

There was a voice message from Mary. She said that a friend of hers, who is vice president of Dardenn's bank, had asked her how solid the earnings forecasts that Ron had provided to them were. She told him that I was the key executive who would make or break those forecasts. The vice president then asked whether I'd be staying with Dardenn for the next five years. She told him that I would definitely stay if the Dardenn brothers didn't push me out.

Just as we reached the apartment, Paul called me, upset. "Mike, a half hour ago, Larry ordered me to change the drawings and when I refused, he fired me. Then he called security and had me escorted from the building. I can't believe they did this to me."

"Larry's a hothead. I'll call Ron right away. Sit tight, I'll call you back."

I reached Ron on the first ring. Before I could say a word, he hammered "Mike, you stay out of this, I warned you about him. I got a call coming in from Delyon" Then he hung up.

Searching for High Leverage and High Meaning

Two minutes later a call came in from Ron. His voice was restrained.

"One of your guys told the people at Delyon that Paul had been fired. If you'd have kept him in line, we wouldn't have this problem. You need to tell him not to talk to Delyon. Period."

"Ron, Larry just fired Paul! Why would he do anything I ask him to do?"

"He listens to you. You tell him to keep his mouth shut!" Ron said.

So much for asking Ron to see Paul's point of view, I thought. I decided to start lower on Maslow's pyramid.

"Ron, hear me out on this. Half of our current sales are new products that were developed in the past five years. We profit eight to ten million dollars per year on products Paul and his group have designed, and their yearly budget is less than a million dollars. If anyone is irreplaceable, it's Paul."

"Bull! He thinks he is."

"What if one of our competitors hired Paul?"

"I'd sue him," he shouted into my ear.

"You can't deprive him of the right to make his living."

"Look, I'll take him back," he said. "But you start looking for someone to replace him. I'll give you six months. But warn him that he'd better play ball."

I interrupted. "Ron, we need to ask him to take us back."

He laughed derisively. "That'll be the day. I'll take him back; end of discussion!"

Building a Bridge

Marcus and I had dinner at Mamma Gina's. We talked and laughed about the old days. It was fun and, for a while, my mind wasn't on Dardenn. But as soon as we had finished dessert, he became serious again.

"Mike, how is the problem at Dardenn going?"

"Well you know that Ron's brother, Larry, has decided that we should remove a critical part from one of our new products. My engineering director didn't agree to change the drawings, and Larry fired him. And it's tough for me to deal with a problem that's thousands of miles away."

"Mike, everyone's focus is on the critical part, which is not a high-leverage opportunity. There have to be high-leverage opportunities out there for Dardenn."

"I tried to get Ron to see the bigger picture. I told him that if we make that change without Delyon's approval, we could lose its business. He doesn't believe that could happen."

"If you did lose Delyon's business, what would that mean to Ron?"

"Ron wants the business to grow beyond what his dad created. He definitely doesn't want to be known as the son who oversaw a decline in the company."

"So Ron's highest meanings are doing better than his father?"

"Definitely," I said.

"That may be the high meaning you're looking for," he said. He took a sip of his cappuccino. "But we also need to find where the high-leverage is. How much stock did you earn during the time when Jesse couldn't pay you?"

"The company was worth very little then. Over those first six years, Jesse couldn't pay me nearly half the time. My unpaid salary amounted to over twenty-eight percent of the stock in the company."

He nodded. "Does that mean if one of the brothers bought your stock, he'd be in control?"

"Intriguing thought," I said. "But I would never pit one brother against the other. I want to do what's best for the people at Dardenn."

"I wasn't suggesting that you sell, merely pointing out that you have high leverage in any negotiation."

We left Mama Gina's and strolled toward the apartment. "Tomorrow morning, before your flight, we'll explore the act of seizing opportunity," he said. "Between finding an opportunity and seizing an opportunity is a great canyon that swallows most opportunity finders. Building a bridge across the canyon is the work of leaders, designers, and implementers. The seizing process is like a military battle. You can plan it and manage it but, once the battle begins, you must lead it."

When we reached the apartment, he shook my hand and said, "I can't think of anyone who's better able to help Dardenn overcome its Goliath. I'll meet you here at six in the morning."

"Thanks," I said. He saluted and left.

Old Eagle Eye

I immediately called Ron. "Ron, you told me you wanted to beat Jesse's five-year growth plan. That's impossible without Paul." I said firmly.

"Okay, okay, you ask him to come back. But I don't ever want to hear one more word about what he won't do. And he had better get his story right for Delyon."

"Ron, look at this from Paul's point of view," I urged. Why would he come back if I asked him? He knows I've lost influence in this company. I told him I'd stop them from eliminating the vent and I couldn't. He knows I can't protect him if you decide to fire him two weeks from now."

"Damn, could you come up with some answers?" Ron asked stridently.

"Ron, trust me on this. Call Paul. Tell him you appreciate what he's done for the company and that Larry made a mistake. Ask him to come back."

There was a long silence. "I could tell him I know that he's a team player. That'll let him know I expect him to help us with Delyon."

I spoke softly, "If you ask Paul to lie, you'll lose him."

Ron was silent again for a moment. "I have to think about this," he finally said.

I wanted to ask him about the bank situation but I couldn't without letting him know that Mary had told me about it. I bit my tongue.

There was message from our production manager, Rick, saying that Larry had ordered them to start moving everything back the way it was years ago, before all the manufacturing improvements were made. He said that Larry had told him it would reduce labor, but he knew it would increase labor and hurt delivery and quality. He said that all the guys had heard about Paul being fired, so they were running around doing whatever Larry wanted.

I left a message on Larry's phone, asking him to call me. Then I called Mary to ask if she had heard anything more from the bank.

"Something's going on, and I don't like it," she said. "When I told Ron that the bank president called and asked for our financials, he told me to supply the information and not to talk to anyone about it. I didn't tell him I'd told you already. Mike, I suspect we're applying for some kind of loan or line of credit. But that doesn't make sense with all the cash reserves we have. I don't like it," she repeated.

"Keep trying to find out all you can," I said.

"You know me, old eagle eye," she said. In my mind, I could see her smiling.

Two Thousand People

Later that evening I called Paul to see if Ron had contacted him.

"Yes, he keeps calling," Paul said. "My wife answers the phone. He told her he wants me back. He's got her working on me."

"Paul, he knows that he needs you. This isn't about him or you. How did you feel when you left Dardenn yesterday?"

"Mike, It killed me to tell my family that I was fired, after all the evenings and weekends I've given that company. We're all in shock. But I'm not going to live like that."

"Ron fired you, but you and I could fire two-thousand people," I said, searching for the higher meaning.

"What?"

"If we don't stay with the company, what do you think will happen to the people who work there?"

There was a long pause. "Mike, I use to think how lucky I was to have a secure job while guys I went to college with were being laid off and fired in all the downsizing and in the outsourcing of jobs overseas. And now I'm on the street after twenty-two years with the company."

"Paul, with your expertise and track record, you'll find great opportunities. But right now the right thing for us to do is to be faithful to the people at Dardenn. Think about what Jessie would want us to do."

After another pause, Paul said. "Okay, the next time Ron calls, I'll talk to him."

Suddenly a worry crossed my mind. Ron was great at selling an opportunity to a cautious customer. But when he believes that people are below him, he doesn't sell, he tells. I cautioned Paul, "Keep in mind that Ron might not say the right things." Then I tried to reach Paul's higher meanings. "This is not about some inappropriate remark he might make; it's about the futures of people who depend on us."

"I understand," he said. It'll be good to see you."

"You too."

An hour later, I received a call from Ron. He said that he had talked to Paul. Sounding pleased with himself, he said that Paul had learned his lesson and was anxious to get his job back. He also said that Delyon wanted to talk to Paul and me and that he had scheduled a meeting in his office at nine o'clock Saturday morning, in order for us to get our stories together. He said that he wanted me to immediately begin to expand our plant in China.

It was another restless night.

Finding & Seizing Great Opportunities

Seize Great Opportunities
12. Develop other innovators and high achievers
11. Deliver rewards
10. Seize rapidly at high-leverage points
9. Use superior design and planning processes

Mobilize Support
8. Find common meaning with and negotiate with opposers
7. Sell the opportunity to those that are cautious
6. Co-create with those eager for opportunity
5. Find the highest meanings of others

Find Great Opportunities
4. Select only high-leverage opportunities
3. Learn to envision opportunities
2. Use powerful learning processes
1. Differentiate yourself for opportunity

PART III

Four Actions to Seize Great Opportunities

To rank as a masterpiece, a work of art must stand as a supreme and timeless accomplishment. Creating one work this extraordinary could be the crowning glory of any artist's life. And among the few who have achieved the remarkable distinction of producing a masterpiece in more than one branch of the arts, Michelangelo Buonarotti stands almost totally alone. His vast number of creations includes the vivid biblical scenes that grace the ceiling of the Sistine Chapel and the heroic marble statue of David. During his own lifetime, he was called divine.

A & E Television Networks: "Biography: Michelangelo, Artist and Man"[79]

At six a.m., I met Marcus in front of the apartment building. I put on my best smile. "It's a fine morning to walk," he said. "I'll continue where we left off.

"As I said last night, between the finding and the seizing of an opportunity is a great canyon that swallows most opportunity finders. I've analyzed how over one hundred great opportunity seizers bridged that canyon. I've broken what they did down to the four most powerful seizing actions:

9. Use superior design and planning processes
10. Seize rapidly at high-leverage points
11. Deliver rewards
12. Develop other innovators and high achievers"

"Seizing opportunity begins with design, and our next leader is a master."

Use Superior Design and Planning Processes

Think of the end before the beginning.

Leonardo da Vinci[80]

"*I*n nineteen fifty-four, Sol Price, a young lawyer, opened a discount store. Everything went well until he discounted bottled alcoholic beverages. He was threatened with jail and hit with a major lawsuit from the alcoholic-beverage industry. He fought back and survived a hurricane of lawsuits. He narrowly escaped jail, but he won against all odds and built a three-hundred-million-dollar chain of stores called FedMart. In nineteen seventy-four, he sold the chain with the agreement that he and his sons would continue as top executives. Within a year, the new owner fired them.

"Price felt betrayed.[81] Nevertheless, as the great ones always did, he searched until he found another opportunity. He found that small retailers couldn't make any profit selling cigarettes, candy, and soft drinks. Wholesalers were charging them a twenty-five-percent markup because their orders were small. Price and his son Robert reasoned that, if they could design a wholesale business that was profitable at a ten-percent markup on small orders, they could capture the small-retailer market."

"After finding the opportunity, Sol and Robert Price used a design process that is used by great designers and anyone who wants to seize opportunities."

"Anyone?" I asked. "A lot of people don't feel capable of design."

"We're natural designers," Marcus said. "Watch a child build with blocks or plan a tea party. That's design. Whether you plant a garden or create a plan to attract investors, you're designing." He looked at me

Café

intently. "We design our lives or they're designed for us. Mike, you're a master designer; you already know how to design. But many opportunity finders fail to seize opportunity because they don't have a good process."

We returned to the café by the bell tower that we had visited on Tuesday. "Best espresso in Florence," Marcus said as he ordered. While we were waiting for our food, he began again. "Once the opportunity has been found, the designer's job is to create whatever is needed—a new product, process, system, or organization—that will fulfill the opportunity. To do this, the designer must answer these questions:

- What is the purpose of the design and who are its beneficiaries?
- How do we create the best design?
- How do we ensure that the design will work?"

"We've studied the processes of the best designers and boiled them down to three phases, each answering one of these questions. A great designer will consider the first question to be the most important one."

What Is The Purpose Of The Design And Who Are Its Beneficiaries?

"The great designer, Leonardo da Vinci, said, 'Always think of the end before the beginning.' Although it may seem obvious that the first phase should focus on the end purpose, often the questions about purpose and beneficiaries are not well-answered before design work begins. Steven Covey[82] identifies 'beginning with the end in mind' as a habit of highly successful people and a guideline for life design."

9. Use superior design and planning processes

- What is the purpose of the design and who are it's beneficiaries?
- How do we create the best design?
- How do we ensure it will work?

"The Prices' end purpose was a business that made a profit providing small orders of name-brand goods, at a ten-percent markup, to small retailers, so they could compete with large retailers. To meet that purpose, their design would have to eliminate credit card fees, costs of giving people credit, shipping-breakdown costs, trucking costs, delivery costs, and outside-sales costs. Also, inventory and leasing costs would have to be low."

"The first phase of design always involves finding the purpose. The award-winning movie maker, Sidney Lumet,[83] has directed over thirty feature films, including *Twelve Angry Men, Serpico, Murder on the Orient Express, The Verdict, The Pawnbroker, and Dog Day Afternoon.* Sidney says his first phase begins with asking the screenwriter: 'What is this story about? What did you see? What was your intention? Ideally, if we do this well, what do you hope the audience will feel, think, sense? In what mood do you want them to leave the theater?' He says the answers to these questions determine how the movie will be cast; how it will look; how it will be made, edited, musically scored, mixed, and titled."

"Before they finish phase one, master designers analyze to be sure the design concept matches the purpose." He riffled through the manuscript. "Here's a list of some checks they use."

Phase-One Checks

❏ *Is the opportunity high leverage?*
❏ *Is there a real or perceived need for what we're designing? Does
    the design have high meaning and high value to customers?*
❏ *Do we have a good estimate of the benefits to the customer?*
❏ *Have we designed the product with enough uniqueness to at-
    tract customers?*
❏ *Do we know the target customers or target market?*
❏ *Have we estimated correctly the size of the target market?*
❏ *Have we covered the right-size market with the design? Have
    we tried to cover too broad a market? Have we designed fea-
    tures into the product or service that have no value to the tar-
    get customers?*
❏ *Have we tested the basic concept or a model of the design with
    potential customers?*

While I looked at the manuscript, Marcus ate. Then he resumed
talking. "As we'll see, Sol initially overestimated the size of the market
for his business."

"Once the designer knows the purpose of the design and its beneficiaries, he or she goes on to answer the second question."

How Do We Create The Best Design?

"In this phase, we must decide what functions the design must perform to meet its purpose and what ideas, patterns, forms, and processes can be combined to provide the new functions and be practical for
implementation..

"Sol and Robert designed not only what functions their business
would perform but also what it would not do. By selling only name
brands that were advertised nationally, they could keep his advertising
costs low. They could trim the costs of receiving, stocking, and inventory by carrying only three thousand brand-name products. A typical
Kmart at that time carried a hundred thousand. Sol said that he set the
limit because 'you can't be everything to everybody.' This wisdom applies to designs of all products and services."

"They also designed what functions the customer would perform. By having customers pay with cash or a check, they could eliminate credit-card fees and accounts-receivable costs. By having customers buy goods in bulk packs, they could eliminate shipping-breakdown costs. By having customers pick up their own merchandise at their warehouse, they could eliminate delivery costs. By placing the warehouse in a low-rent area, they could keep overhead costs low."

"In the second phase, most designers use new technology only when the new technology is proven and is needed to create the best design. Sol Price didn't need new technologies, such as computer programs and automated warehouses, to make his initial design meet his purpose. Great designers first try forms or processes that fit existing technologies."

"Developing new technology often takes large resources and long times. Saturn succeeded in designing a new car, a new factory, and new manufacturing processes; shaping a new workforce and management philosophy; developing new suppliers; creating a new distribution system; and fundamentally improving the way in which cars are sold. But it took seven years and it cost Saturn billions before it became profitable. Only a company like General Motors could have financed it."

"When Honda moved to the U.S., it duplicated a car, a process, and a factory it already had in Japan. It carefully selected a workforce and suppliers that it felt would readily adopt Japanese manufacturing methods. It sent workers to Japan to learn the process. It was up and running profitably in less than two years."

"Many designers fail when they try to do too much in the second phase."

Optimize the Whole: Zoom in, Zoom out

"In the second phase," Marcus said between bites, "great designers optimize the whole. Frederick Brooks,[84] the chief designer of IBM's Three Sixty, the most successful mainframe computer of all time, says that unity of design is the most important design consideration. To achieve unity of design, 'the overall design must meet the intent or purpose of the opportunity' and 'each part should be aligned and designed in best relationship to each other and to the purpose of the overall design.'"

"Master designers do not optimize the whole by optimizing the parts. They first optimize the whole and then they optimize the parts to fit the optimum whole. To do this, they begin at the highest level, then move rapidly from upper levels of the design to lower levels and back to upper levels. This ensures that the forms and functions of the smaller components of the design fit the overall design, and vice versa. Edison could think one moment of providing power from a massive electrical distribution system; the next moment of the design of the generator that would be needed to create the power; and, a moment later, of a design detail in the rotor of the generator. Master designers move up and down across the various levels of a design as often as fifty times per hour.[85] I call this 'zoom in, zoom out,'" he said.

"Sol Price, Marie Curie, and Michelangelo all could see the forest one moment, a small leaf on a single tree the next moment, and switch back to the forest in the next moment."

"The third phase answers the question: "How do we ensure that the design will work?' It consists of experimental test, analysis, and redesign."

How Do We Ensure That The Design Will Work?

"Sol and Robert rented an abandoned airplane hanger, put shelves in it, put a checkout counter at one end, and named it Price Club. They purchased name-brand items in bulk. They had suppliers deliver them and put them on the shelves. They had shoppers load their own items off the shelves, bring them to the counter, pay cash, and carry them out. Robert Price came up with the idea to sell annual memberships for twenty-five dollars, causing Wall Street analyst Michael Exstein to remark, 'It was unimaginable, this idea that you could charge people to shop.'"

"As with many designers who venture into the unknown, their first test proved that their design didn't work. In its first year, Price Club could not attract enough customers to be profitable and it lost so much money that Sol was threatened with bankruptcy.

"With time and money running out, Sol analyzed what was wrong with the design. He concluded that the design of the store, the product selection, and the cost structure were right. He admitted that his decision to sell only to retailers was killing the business. At bankruptcy's door, the Prices changed the design. They opened the store to government employees and self-employed individuals. The chance to buy wholesale goods through their business and use them personally was irresistible to self-employed people, and Price Club was stampeded with applications. By nineteen eighty-one, sales had reached two hundred thirty million dollars."

"Within ten years, the Prices had twenty-five stores generating two-point-six billion dollars per year. Their design was so successful that Sam Walton copied it and called it Sam's Club. Sam Walton said, 'I've stolen or borrowed as many ideas from Sol Price as from anybody else.'[86] Pace, Macro, and Costco also copied the design, and Price Club merged with Costco in nineteen ninety-four.

"The second and third phases of the design process often are repeated until the design meets the purpose and is easier to implement. Occasionally, it may be necessary to return to phase one and modify the original purpose, as Sol Price did."

General Principles of Experimental Testing

Marcus moved his plate to one side and continued, "A general principle of experimental design and testing that great designers use is: Early in the design process, identify the high-risk parts of the design and redesign to eliminate the risk. Then test the new designs under the worst conditions and make corrections."

"The earlier in the design process that you test a design, the better. The IDEO[87] Corporation leads the world in industrial design. Its designs range from high-tech blood analyzers to stand-up toothpaste tubes. Once it understands the market, the technology, and the constraints on the problem, IDEO observes people in real situations in that market, to find out what makes them tick—what confuses them, what they like, what they hate, and where they have latent needs not addressed by current products and services. IDEO designers visualize people using the product and then build a series of quick prototypes to evaluate the design in the hands of customers. General manager Tom Kelley says they try not to get attached to the first few prototypes because they know they'll change."

I said, "At Dardenn, we build models of the product as early as possible to test them. With that, and some of the other early-learning processes you taught us, we shortened our time to develop new products by fifty percent. That helped us keep our position as the new-product leader in our market."

"You've done well, Mike," Marcus said. "Master designers spend a great deal of time imagining what can go wrong with the design. Then they focus on the worst possible failures and design test processes and equipment that will stress the design in a way that induces the failures. They put early models of the design through the tests and they find and fix the defects. They conduct reviews with potential investors—especially customers—to get feedback. The best designers eliminate almost all problems they discover in the test process before they finalize a design."

"Because of the importance of 'early test and build,' many organizations have completely redesigned the first processes in their product-development cycles. The Powertrain Division of General Motors has developed very sophisticated computer-design programs that allow it to design engine components on the computer and then test them on the computer under simulated conditions. It also has developed new processes that allow it to build a first prototype of an engine part in hours, rather than weeks or months. Powertrain then measures and tests these rapidly made prototypes to correct any design defects before finalizing the design. As a result, the quality of GM's engines has greatly improved over the past ten years."

Find Opportunity First

"I want to emphasize a point I made yesterday," Marcus said. The best designers always search for and find a great opportunity first, because identifying problems and solving them is low-leverage activity unless you know that those problems are preventing you from seizing the opportunity.[88] Then the best designers focus only on problems that stand in the way of seizing great opportunities."

Thinking Skills

"Great designers use thinking skills, such as imagining, synthesizing, testing, and analyzing, in all phases of their design and problem-solving processes. Can you see where Sol and Robert Price used them to find and seize a wholesale business opportunity?"

I nodded and said, "Synthesis, or putting parts

> **Analyze:** Examine the parts of a whole to determine their natures, functions, forms, fits, and relationships to one another and to the whole.
>
> **Synthesize:** Combine parts or elements to form a coherent whole.

together to form a functional whole, is the most difficult thinking skill to learn."

"Yes," he agreed, "it's one matter to analyze what makes an automobile work; it is far more difficult to synthesize hundreds of parts into a well-performing machine."

"What do you recommend to someone who wants to improve his or her thinking skills?" I asked.

"*The Teaching of Thinking,*[89] by Nickerson, is a good review of the research on thinking skills. But, as I said before, the highest-leverage way to learn anything is in the pursuit of future opportunity. So work with a great opportunity finder if you can. Engage in a project requiring design and problem solving, and work with a good problem solver on the project."

Meta-cognition

"Researchers[90] have found that expert designers and problem solvers monitor and question their own thinking processes while they are thinking. This is called meta-cognition and it can be learned. At first, you have to force it to happen by interrupting yourself regularly with questions. When I'm helping a group to search for opportunities, I interrupt occasionally with questions that challenge the direction of our thinking. Here are some questions I use," he said, pointing to a page in the manuscript.

Meta-cognitive Questions

- ❏ *Have we found the highest-leverage opportunity?*
- ❏ *Have we defined the future state we are seeking and the gap between it and the present state?*
- ❏ *Do we know the highest-leverage problems we must solve?*
- ❏ *Have we defined the results we want from the solutions? Are our assumptions correct?*
- ❏ *Are we on track in solving the problem, and is there a better problem-solving technique?*
- ❏ *Have we subdivided the problem correctly? Have we explored optional solutions?*
- ❏ *Have we found the highest-leverage solution?*

"When the design work is completed, implementation begins," he went on. "To achieve the full potential of the design, we should focus resources—such as people, money, and expertise—at high-leverage points. A high-leverage point is a point at which we can spend a small amount of resources to produce large benefits. This is the next seizing action."

"Each of us can recall a moment in his or her life when a different decision or a different choice would have led to an entirely different future. So it was with Bill Gates in the summer of nineteen eighty."

Seize Rapidly at High-Leverage Points

Often, leverage follows the economy of means: where the best results come not from large-scale efforts, but from small well-focused actions.

Peter Senge[91]

"In nineteen eighty, IBM decided to build a personal computer," Marcus said. "It also decided that, to get it to the market fast with a competitive cost, it would have to be built with components and software obtained from outside IBM. Jack Sams was given the job of finding software suppliers. Sams knew that Microsoft, a small company with thirty-two employees, supplied most of the software for personal computers on the market. So he called Bill Gates, the president of Microsoft, and asked for a meeting. Gates said, 'How about two weeks?' Sams said, 'How about tomorrow?'

"The next day, Sams flew to Bellevue, Washington. As he exited an elevator at Microsoft, he was met by what appeared to be an awkward, teenaged office boy in a poorly fitting suit. The boy kept pushing his dirty, wire-rimmed glasses up on his nose. Sams soon discovered that this was Gates. Gates rocked back and forth during the meeting, appearing to be scatterbrained. Microsoft's offices were tiny by IBM standards; they didn't make a good first impression. IBM asked Gates to sign a nondisclosure agreement; Gates signed without hesitation."

"In a three-hour meeting, Gates impressed Sams with his grasp of PC hardware, software, and the industry. Sams said that Gates was one of the smartest people he ever met."

Sams told Gates he wanted him to provide the disc-operating system for the new computer. Gates surprised Sams by saying he didn't supply operating systems and referring him to DRI, which had a popular operating system at that time.

"When IBM's people visited DRI, DRI's president was unavailable, and his business manager refused to sign the nondisclosure agreement, so, under IBM's rules of engagement, there could be no discussion. After hours of stalemate, the IBM representatives left.

"Sams called Gates again and told him that Microsoft had to supply an operating system or IBM wouldn't buy Microsoft's language programs. Gates felt that operating systems were not his expertise and that developing an operating system would pull resources away from where Microsoft made its money. Besides, if Microsoft entered the operating-system business, DRI might react by entering the language business.

"However, pressed with an ultimatum, Gates decided to do it. He knew another developer who had an operating system. A visit with the other developer confirmed that he would sell his operating system. Gates immediately called Sams to tell him he had it. They discussed whether Microsoft or IBM should buy it. It's not clear whether either of them knew the significance of the ownership of that piece of software. It was decided that Microsoft[92] would buy it, and that decision ultimately drove Microsoft's stock value to four hundred billion dollars. For Gates and Sams, this was a defining moment, a high-leverage point in time."

"Sams believed that, if IBM bought the software, it would bungle it, and he wanted Microsoft to be responsible for integrating all the software. Gates wanted to be known as the company that supplied IBM's personal-computer software. He knew that was a high-leverage opportunity and that the purchase of the operating system was a high-leverage point, so he bought the software for fifty thousand dollars—a lot of money at that time."

"Referring to this leverage point, the writer-analyst Paul Carrol said, 'Sams may be right that IBM would have bungled DOS (disk operating system), but IBM, in not being able to seize that chance, put themselves at a horrible disadvantage.'"[93]

I said, "In defense of Sams, leverage points are fleeting; you have to act quickly, and if he had brought the DOS inside IBM, that probably would have delayed IBM's introduction of the PC by at least a year."

"True," Marcus said. "There would be other high-leverage points on Microsoft's journey and, nearly every time, Gates took the right action at the right moment. Later, Gates sold nonexclusive rights to IBM to use the DOS software. IBM was confident that the software was useless without a special chip it had designed into the computer. Later, Compaq Computer reverse-engineered the IBM chip and produced an IBM clone. As others developed clones, Microsoft sold them DOS software. Eventually, DOS became Windows, the standard software on most of the world's personal computers."

"Later, IBM spent hundreds of millions of dollars suing Compaq and Microsoft, trying to reclaim the DOS software that Microsoft had bought. IBM lost nearly every suit. At the time of the leverage point, Microsoft had thirty-two employees and a few million dollars in sales, and IBM had three hundred forty thousand employees and twenty-six billion dollars in sales. But Microsoft had the inside-expertise and was led by Gates, a master of high-leverage opportunity and high-leverage points."

"Isn't this also an example of a power-insider hiring an expertise-insider?" I asked.

"Yes," he answered. "The irony is that IBM got the expertise but Gates got the power.

"To learn how to find and seize opportunities using high-leverage points, the leader must answer these questions:
- What is a high-leverage point?
- How do we find high-leverage points?
- How do we act at multiple points in an organized campaign?"

10. Seize rapidly at high-leverage points
- What is a high-leverage point?
- How do we find high-leverage points?
- How do we act at multiple points in an organized campaign?

What Is A High-leverage Point?

"A high-leverage point is a point in a system where a small action produces a large change in the operation and output of the system. There are many varieties of high-leverage points, from the up-button in an elevator to a bottleneck in a manufacturing process. Learning to find high-leverage points is both a science and an art."

"An Indianapolis Five Hundred race car has small wings on each side at the front. Indy winner Bobby Rahal says that changing the angle on the left-front aerodynamic wing by one-tenth of one degree might get you around the Speedway one-tenth of a second faster. At the end of two hundred laps at Indianapolis, that's a difference of twenty seconds, enough to win or lose the race. Rahal says that if you can figure out enough of these minute adjustments so that you can gain a few seconds per lap, you can run away with the Indy Five Hundred. The angle of each wing is a high-leverage point," Marcus explained, "because a very small change in the angle makes a large difference in the outcome of the race."

How Do We Find High-leverage Points?

"To repeat, a high-leverage point is a point where we can spend a small amount of resources to produce large benefits. Peter Senge,[94] who has researched the dynamics of systems, says, 'the areas of highest leverage are often the least obvious.' For example, a very large force is needed to change the direction of a moving ship, if you are pushing its front in the direction in which you want it to go. But a small force to change the angle of the rudder will turn the ship. The rudder is an example of an obvious leverage point. However, the tiny trim tab on a ship is a not-so-obvious leverage point. An even smaller change in the position of the trim tab increases or decreases how much effort it will take to move the rudder.

"Because of the great value of high-leverage points, it's very important to learn how to find them. I'll give you several examples."

Edison, Another Master of Leverage Points

"In the movie, *Edison the Man,* Spencer Tracy, playing Edison, is sitting at his desk early one morning, after struggling through the night trying to find a suitable filament. He is holding a piece of sewing thread in his hand. 'We're going to use carbon,' he says to the men just coming to work. After he gives instructions to one of the men about how to impregnate the thread with carbon and bake it, the man says, 'It's too delicate, Tom, I'm afraid we'll break it.' 'Try it anyway,' Edison says. Another man says, 'But we've tried carbon before.' 'Not carbonized thread,' Edison says. 'That isn't very scientific,' the man says. 'I told you we had to leave science behind. Now come on,' Tom says, motioning for them to get on with it."

Thomas Edison

"They prepare the thread as Edison has instructed and, lo and behold, although all previous filaments had burned out in minutes, the lamp burns continually through that night and the following night. In that dramatic moment, Edison gives the world the gift of electric lighting."

"This story reinforces the myth that breakthroughs come magically. As I've said before, we've been led to believe that if we simply free the imaginative and playful children's minds within us, we will be able to create visions.

"On the contrary, before Edison built the first filaments for his lamp, his physicist, Upton, already had determined that the filament must have an electrical resistance of around one hundred ohms, a melting point over six thousand degrees Fahrenheit, and be extremely thin and long without being too fragile. The eventual focus on carbon was no accident, in that Edison knew its properties and had worked with it in developing an improved telephone voice-piece. But even after his team narrowed the search to extremely thin carbon filaments, the search lasted for the best part of eighteen seventy-nine."

"Edison and his team mentally 'saw' their solutions long before they ever realized them in the laboratory. This narrowed the scope from millions of experiments to thousands. In other words, they knew millions of things that wouldn't work, so they didn't need to try them. Long before the 'magical' experiment took place, they knew which materials and which experiments were the highest leverage."

Marcus pulled his manuscript out of what appeared to be a very old messenger bag that he was carrying over his shoulder. He turned to a page, and handed it to me, saying, "In that drawing, you can follow Edison's leverage-point focus. At the top, I list the high-leverage opportunity he found—a commercial electrical lighting system. He knew that he would

Edison's High Leverage Point Focus

High-Leverage Opportunity

Commercially successful lighting system using electricity insted of gas

Major Developments Needed

A high capacity power source
A suitable lamp
A practical distribution system

Highest-leverage development
A Suitable lamp

Problems with Lamp

Invent a practical socket
Invent a high resistance, durable lamp
Invent a filament mounting support
Invent a vacuum enclosure

Highest-leverage problem
Invent a high resistance, high temperature, durable filament

Actions needed to find best filament material

Search for tough carbon-based materials
Design, build, mount, and enclose filaments
Test filaments

Highest-leverage action
Design, build, mount, and vacuum enclose filaments

have to develop all the parts of the generators, lamps, and distribution system. Of these developments, he knew that finding a suitable lamp was the high-leverage development and that the major problem would be inventing a high-resistance, high-temperature, yet durable filament. Finally, he knew that the highest-leverage action was to design, build, and mount the filaments and create vacuums around them."

"Realizing the importance of the highest-leverage action, Edison invented a self-contained, fast-turnaround laboratory to do it. He staffed it with chemists who could carbonize his filaments, physicists who could calculate from the properties of materials whether they had a chance of working, an expert on high vacuum, a glass blower, and an expert on glass-to-metal seals. The team could start with an idea for a filament in the morning, build it that afternoon, and test it that evening. The scientists were able to test thousands of materials, filament cross sections, and carbonizing techniques, dozens of vacuum methods and glass-to-metal seals, and hundreds of wire supports for the filaments."

"Two years after he started his lighting project, Edison ran out of money." Marcus paused and continued, "Just as they found the answer. If he hadn't searched for the highest leverage in the beginning, he never would have made it. Rather than two years, it would have taken ten years to develop a suitable filament.

"So the search for high-leverage points begins once we have a vision of a great opportunity. Starting at the highest level of the opportunity, we systematically work our way down, level by level, selecting the highest-leverage points at each level. Then, to make sure we have identified a genuine high-leverage point, we need to ask whether a small change at that point will make a large difference in our ability to seize the high-level opportunity. Edison knew that if his team could invent a suitable filament, he could create a commercially successful electric lighting system. We need to understand the leverage point well enough to perform the right action on it. The question for you is, 'Where are the leverage points in your struggle with Larry and Ron?'"

"That's exactly what I was wondering," I said.

"You'll find them." Marcus then continued his story. "Churchill also was a master of leverage-point decisions, especially in crisis. Two of his most important decisions at leverage points took place shortly after he became the Prime Minister of England."[95]

Crisis Leverage Points and Winston Churchill

"The first decision came just as Hitler's armored divisions invaded France. The French begged Churchill for British fighter planes to help in their defense. Churchill believed that the French would lose, even with British fighter support, and that the planes would be needed to defend Britain. He said 'no.' In other words, he decided that it would be a low-leverage action. He was proved right when Hitler began his air attack of Britain. Without the planes, Britain wouldn't have withstood Hitler's massive bombing attack."

"A second, difficult, leverage-point decision was necessary when France surrendered to Germany. Churchill did not want the French Navy to fall into German hands, so he asked the French Admiral to either join the British Navy or demobilize his ships. When the Admiral refused, the British Navy seized all French ships in British waters and sank or disabled all the other French ships it could find. Churchill recognized this as a high-leverage point because the Germans would reap a large benefit from the French ships, and only a small amount of British resources was required to seize or sink them."

Leverage Points of Expertise

"John Browne, the CEO of British Petroleum, insists that 'everyone in the company who is not directly accountable for a profit be involved in creating and distributing knowledge the company can use to make a profit.'[96] He says, 'the key to reaping a big return is to leverage knowledge by sharing it throughout the company so each unit is not learning in isolation.'"

"To expand on Browne's idea, consider expertise as a valuable resource. Then consider that, when learning takes place in one part of an organization, a great deal of the investment to learn already has been made. A leverage point of expertise is any place in an organization where known expertise can be applied to get large benefits."

Leverage Points in Time

I said, "At Dardenn, when we lay out a project, we shorten the time it takes to finish it by having planners find the path in the project that takes the longest time and then work to reduce the time on that path. Your way of looking at leverage points is to say that any event on the longest time line is a high-leverage point because it holds up the whole project."

"If it holds up the whole project, it should be treated like open-heart surgery."

"Open-heart surgery?" I asked.

"During open-heart surgery, a critical time is when the chest cavity is open and blood is being bypassed around the heart," he explained. "What would be an acceptable reason to interrupt the surgeon during this time: taking a non-emergency call from his daughter, or his stockbroker, or from a racquetball buddy who wants to arrange a match?"

I smiled at his examples.

"When a major portion of the project is held up until an action is finished, we should use the rules for the surgeon when the chest cavity is open," he said.

"If I did that, I'd ask the engineer working on the critical path to stay all night."

"Edison, Gates, and Smith worked all night with the person at the high-leverage point," he said. "When Curie knew she was onto something, she worked nonstop."

I shook my head. "If I carried that to the extreme, I'd be at work twenty-four hours a day, seven days a week."

"Any good concept can be carried too far," he said. "However, in this fast-paced world, I teach the open-heart-surgery principle and many other models and concepts to companies that want to reduce product-development time and time to market."[97]

Leverage Points in Battle

"In nineteen forty, the freedom of the world was threatened as Hitler rolled his war machine across Europe. He seemed unstoppable. On December seventh, nineteen forty-three, U.S. President Franklin Delano Roosevelt flew to Tunis, North Africa, where he was whisked from his plane and placed in General Eisenhower's car. As the car drove off, he turned to Eisenhower and said, 'Ike, you're going to command Overlord.' Overlord was the code word for the Invasion of Normandy—history's greatest sea-to-land battle."

"Throughout his life, Eisenhower was chosen to lead important missions. Why?"

"Because he had a high batting average of successful missions?" I ventured.

"Yes, he was not only well-prepared for opportunity;[98] he almost always delivered great returns to investors in the mission. Eisenhower delivered because his thinking was both high leverage and high meaning."

"His high-leverage thinking can be seen in the way in which the invasion was planned. He knew that attacks from sea to land are inherently difficult and generally unsuccessful. Although he had commanded successful, large-scale, sea-to-land operations in North Africa, Sicily, and Salerno, these were not direct frontal attacks from the sea against highly fortified land positions.[99] So he knew he had to find high-leverage points."

"The Germans had constructed a seemingly impenetrable wall of fortified gun bunkers along the French coast. The shores were heavily mined. On the other side of the wall were twenty divisions of battle-hardened, heavily armed, highly mobile Panzers, under the command of the legendary Field Marshall, Erwin Rommel.[100] The Germans could launch a massive counterattack with over one hundred thousand troops within days of the first attack.[101] Behind all that were six hundred thousand, heavily armed, German troops, allocated to defend France."

"Eisenhower knew that, to win over superior forces, he had to concentrate his forces, act with speed, be mobile, and surprise the enemy Because the Germans had to defend over three thousand five hundred miles of coastline, running from Holland to the southern end of the

President Dwight D. Eisenhower

Bay of Biscay,[102] they had to spread their forces widely. The Allies could concentrate their forces on a small part of the coastline and surprise the Germans. The Allies chose five beaches on the Normandy coast as high-leverage points."

"Because most high-leverage points exist only in narrow windows of time, they must be seized quickly," Marcus continued. "Eisenhower knew that the invading troops would be outnumbered six to one if Rommel were able to move his full force toward Normandy. Ike decided to decrease the mobility and speed of Rommel's divisions by bombing all the railroads and bridges behind Rommel's forces. This would isolate them from their supply lines. Ike also decided that the Allies would bomb Rommel's tanks if he moved them forward. These were high-leverage-point bombings."

> *Since the focus of effort represents our bid for victory, we must direct it at that object which will cause the most decisive damage to the enemy and which holds the best opportunity of success. . . . It forces us to concentrate decisive combat power just as it forces us to accept risk. Thus, we focus our effort against critical enemy vulnerability, exercising strict economy elsewhere.*
>
> From *Warfighting: The US Marine Corps Book of Strategy*[103]

"However, the air forces were not under Eisenhower's command. The generals who headed the air forces believed that strategic bombing of German industry and terror bombing of German cities would end the war, and that Overlord was not necessary. Eisenhower believed that these views were dangerous nonsense—that a fanatical, resolved Hitler would fight to the death and would have to be defeated on the ground. Hitler proved Eisenhower right."

"Convinced that bombing prior to and during the invasion was essential and high-leverage, Eisenhower gambled his career on it. In London, he told the combined chiefs of staff, 'Every obstacle must be overcome, every inconvenience suffered, and every risk run to ensure that our blow is decisive. We cannot afford to fail.' He threatened to step down from the position of commander-in-chief if he weren't given the support of the air commands." Marcus paused. "Eisenhower got his air support, and it would be clear later to everyone, including the objecting air commanders, that he was right. He had seen what others didn't see and was willing to stake his career on it."

How Do We Act At Multiple Points In An Organized Campaign?

"When the great achievers found high-leverage points, they organized teams and designed action plans to act on all the points available, in a timely, coordinated way," Marcus said. Eisenhower and his staff divided the overall mission into smaller, coordinated missions that were focused on high-leverage points. In the manuscript is an example of the overall Overlord mission and a small, coordinated mission at a high-leverage point.[104] He took the manuscript, turned some pages, and pushed it back toward me."

Mission of entire Allied Expeditionary Force before the invasion of Normandy: You will enter the continent of Europe and, in conjunction with the other United Nations, undertake operations aimed at the heart of Germany and the destruction of her armed forces. After adequate channel ports have been secured, secure an area that will facilitate both ground and air operations against the enemy.

High-leverage-point mission assigned to England's 6th Airborne Division of paratroopers during the invasion: Land on the eastern end of the beachhead near Caen. Once there, carry out the following tasks: secure crossings over the Orne River and Caen Canal, knock out big coastal guns in the area, and block German reinforcements from reaching the Allied troops landing on the beaches.

"All the high-leverage points were acted on in a well-timed, well-executed invasion. In the early hours of the invasion, special forces were dropped behind the enemy's lines to direct massive naval guns that would pound the German fortifications just before the first troops landed. Commando teams were dropped in by gliders and by parachute to blow up key bridges and secure important positions. Thousands of individual missions at high-leverage points were planned and timed to support the main thrust, the landing at five beaches on the Normandy coast."

"Acting at many high-leverage points in an organized, timely way increases the probability that we'll achieve large returns, even if action

Acting at High-Leverage Points Increases Chances of Success

When resources are applied at many high-leverage points, benefits are high even if one leverage point fails to produce or there are unexpected losses.

at one of the high-leverage points fails or if we have high, unexpected losses, such as those the American forces suffered at Omaha Beach, a code name for one of the beaches." Marcus reached over and turned to another page in the manuscript. This drawing shows how this increases our chances of success."

"I agree with this," I said, "unless you're blocked at a critical leverage point."

"That's a good point," Marcus said. "We should have backup plans for the critical points. Risk is reduced by planning well, by assessing risks at critical points, by taking preemptive action if possible, and by focusing at high-leverage points. When we put a small amount of resources at a high-leverage point, we minimize losses if it doesn't pay off. If it does pay off, the benefits are high."

"It works the same way in new-product introductions and construction projects," I said.

"Yes," he agreed. He continued, "Eisenhower also delivered because he was a high-meaning thinker."

High-Meaning Thinking at High-Leverage Points

"From his past combat leadership, Eisenhower knew that the success of the invasion of Normandy depended heavily on the front wave of soldiers. If the soldiers came storming out of the landing crafts and attacked the enemy, the invasion would succeed. If they cowered behind the landing crafts, the invasion would fail.

"So Eisenhower spent his evenings and weekends with soldiers that were part of the first assaults. He said that every soldier who risks his life should know why, and he should see, face to face, the man who was leading him into battle.[105] In the four months before D-Day, Ike visited twenty-six divisions; twenty-four airfields; five ships; and countless depots, shops, and hospitals. He gave a short speech at each site about defending the future freedom of all people. He said that the men were fighting for their loved ones back home and for the lives they would return to when the war was over. Then he made the rounds, shaking hands and asking questions. Whereas other generals asked the men about their military specialties, training, units, or weapons, Eisenhower asked them, 'Where are you from?' 'What did you do back home?' 'What are your plans for when the war is over?' 'Who's waiting back home for you?' To other generals, these were soldiers. To Eisenhower, they were citizen-soldiers, caught up in a war that none of them wanted. He knew that what meant the most to them were those they had left behind."

"Stories of his inspiring conversations with the men quickly spread through the camps after he left. The troops knew that Eisenhower saw war from their eyes, that he knew what really had meaning for them. As you know, the soldiers in the Normandy invasion fought valiantly. The invasion was so successful that Soviet Premier Joseph Stalin, who seldom praised anyone or anything, said, 'The history of war does not know of an undertaking comparable to it for breadth of conception, grandeur of scale, and mastery of execution.'

"Here are the questions I ask myself to be sure I have a high-leverage action plan for seizing an opportunity," Marcus said, turning over a page in the manuscript as I held it.

Questioning the Plan for Seizing a Great Opportunity

❑ *Is it organized in high-leverage thrusts? Does each thrust have the optimum resources?*

❑ *Are the critical high-leverage points identified along with their risks? Have backup or contingency plans been developed?*

> ❑ *Do we have the resources to carry it out? Have we planned and committed resources at the high-leverage points?*
> ❑ *Is there a detailed plan that specifies actions, resource applications, timing, assignment of responsibilities, and measures of success? Has each person who has a stake in the opportunity accepted responsibility for his or her assigned actions?*
> ❑ *Are events timed to minimize total implementation time and total resource consumption, while maximizing the final outcome?*

Marcus paid the waiter and picked up the manuscript. We took a short break.

I checked my cell phone. There was a text message marked "urgent" from Mary, asking me to call her. I reached her on the first ring. Her voice was strained. "Mike, Larry just announced that he's permanently taking your place as president and that you're going to China to expand our new plant there. He told everyone not to tell you until Ron had a chance to see you after you got back."

I felt betrayed. For twenty-five years, I had helped Jesse Dardenn build Dardenn Corporation from nothing. Now his two boys were pushing me out.

"It'll be okay," I said to Mary in the most convincing voice I could muster. I finished the conversation by thanking her for letting me know and telling her that I was leaving for home in the morning and that I would deal with it when I got back. I decided not to confront Ron until we were face to face.

When Marcus returned, I put on my best smile. We left the café and began to walk at a leisurely pace. Marcus said, "One last thought on seizing opportunity: If a great opportunity or threat exists, it's only a matter of time before other great achievers will find it and seize it. If we don't prepare for, find, and seize the great opportunities that come our way, we suffer the costs of lost opportunities and the loss of potential return on our time, ideas, energy, and resources."

ACTION 11.

Deliver Rewards

*It has been proven time and time again that the only leader
whom soldiers will reliably follow when their lives are on the line
is the leader who is both competent and whom soldiers believe is
committed to their well-being.*

Peter Senge[106]

"The next action is to lead investors to seize the opportunity and the rewards," Marcus said. "This sets the great leaders apart. They know the answer to these questions:
- Why are some leaders chosen to lead over and over again?
- How do we ensure that shareholders will invest again?"

Why Are Some Leaders Chosen To Lead Again And Again?

"Great leaders are chosen to lead again because they deliver rewards to stakeholders. There was no one more determined to deliver rewards to investors than General Eisenhower. He had to deliver to the U.S. Congress, the Joint Chiefs of Staff, his field commanders, his troops, Roosevelt, Churchill, Stalin, and the people in the Allied countries. His desire to

11. Deliver rewards
- Why are some leaders chosen to lead again and again?
- How do we ensure that stakeholders will invest again?

deliver stood out when Walter Cronkite interviewed him twenty years after the invasion of Normandy. Eisenhower said little about the battles, the commanders, the politicians, or the strategies. Instead, he spoke of the men who died in the war, who never enjoyed their grandchildren—whom he didn't deliver for."

"When the war ended, Eisenhower returned to the U.S. as a hero. When he spoke to a joint session of Congress, he received the longest standing ovation in the history of the Congress. He was persuaded to enter politics and went on to serve two terms as President of the United States. Eisenhower was chosen to lead time and time again because he led investors to seize great opportunities and he made sure that the benefits of the opportunities were delivered to the investors."

"Great leaders deliver even when times are tough. In nineteen eighty-six, when FedEx shut down its Zapmail program, it found other jobs in the company for those affected.[107] When it discontinued some operations in Europe, it placed full-page ads urging other employers to hire its workers. In Belgium, eighty companies responded with six hundred job offers. Loyalty in hard times builds a trust fund that pays long-term dividends. Fred Smith believes that, if you take care of your people, they will take care of your customers, the company will be profitable, and your people will have secure futures."

"I have an example of failure to deliver," I said. "For years, companies like IBM AT&T, and GE rewarded loyal employees by assuring them lifetime job security. But, when business went bad and Wall Street rewarded companies that made job cuts, the companies laid off people."

"Yes," Marcus said. "On the other hand, I've worked with a corporation in Chicago that has delivered to employees by never having a layoff in its sixty-five-year history. Its employees are willing to create improvements because they know they won't lose their jobs as a result. They have improved manufacturing-labor productivity by six percent per year for the last five years and have improved customer-delivery response by ten to one. The CEO of the company feels responsible for delivering to the people he leads."

How Do We Ensure That Shareholders Will Invest Again?

Marcus continued, "The key to ensuring that shareholders will invest again is to deliver what means the most to them."

"Great leaders deliver," he said. "In eighteen eighty-one, the government of France awarded Louis Pasteur a medal for developing the vaccines and the antiseptic concepts I discussed earlier. But Pasteur said he would refuse the medal unless the government also gave awards to his research assistants. Many chose to be led by Pasteur because he delivered the benefits."

"Bill Gates has delivered to the employees who helped him to build Microsoft," I said. "He's created more employee millionaires than anyone else in history."

"True," Marcus replied. "Successful leaders respect the expertise and resources of stakeholders and feel responsible for seeing that their investment is rewarded. Stakeholders judge leaders by what they deliver, not what they promise. If they don't deliver, stakeholders may not willingly invest again. Stakeholders seem to know the old saying: I can't hear what you're saying because what you are doing is so loud!"[108]

"Marcus, if I ever needed to deliver, it's now."

He nodded. "You will," he said.

Personal Success Versus Organizational Success

After a few moments, he continued. "When it comes to delivery, noted researcher Jim Collins says that the most successful executives put the organization's success ahead of their own.[109] He says that they go beyond effective leadership. They build the organization's enduring greatness through a mix of humility and professional will."

"Are you saying that the goal of great leaders isn't personal success?" I asked.

"Of course it is," he said. "We all are inclined to put our personal successes first, rather than the contributions we can make to others. However, people such as Edison, Smith, Einstein, Curie, Walton, and Michelangelo achieved personal success as a result of the important contributions they made to others."

"Are you saying that, if a person puts personal success first, he or she is less likely to achieve greatness?" I asked.

"Not always, but in free societies, those who delivered great benefits to stakeholders were more successful personally."

Overview Of First Eleven Actions

"As an overview," he said, "the great leader leads others to find great opportunity; energizes them to willingly invest their time, ideas, and resources; leads them to seize the opportunity; and delivers the benefits to them. If stakeholders believe that they have received good value for their investments, such as personal growth, security, the opportunity to create, social recognition, financial success, a better society, or food for the soul, they'll invest again in opportunities the leader helps them find. And the leader will be chosen to lead again."

"Mike, great innovators and achievers not only deliver, they also develop others so that they, too, can find and seize the great opportunities of their time. Developing other innovators and high achievers is the highest level of leadership, and many can't reach it. I have an example of a brilliant, ambitious man who failed because he fell short of this level."

Develop Innovators and High Achievers

Leaders with a proven track record of success take direct responsibility for the development of other leaders.

Noel M. Tichy[110]

"In nineteen forty-five, radios, telephone circuits, and transmitters built with vacuum tubes were heavy, bulky, expensive, and unreliable, and they required a lot of power to operate. So Bell Labs, the research division of AT&T, formed a scientific team to find a replacement for the vacuum tube. The company appointed William Shockley to lead the team."

"Shockley knew that the person who invented a replacement device would lead a revolution in electronics, computers, and communication systems. Shockley had an idea, and, for a year and a half, two scientists, John Bardeen and Walter Brattain, tried to make Shockley's idea work. Bardeen created hundreds of designs, and Brattain built them and tested them. They all failed. From the failures, Bardeen developed a theory that led them in another direction."

"Following Bardeen's theory, late in December of nineteen forty-seven, Brattain positioned a tiny, V-shaped probe against the surface of a small piece of Germanium. He saw an unexpected signal on the screen of his oscilloscope. He blurted out, 'This thing's got gain,' for everyone in the quiet laboratory to hear. After Bardeen quickly made some calculations, the team members knew they had found a new phenomenon. Their activity increased to a feverish pace. Within a month, they had a working device that eventually was called a transistor."

"Shockley was furious when they told him that they had discovered how to replace the vacuum tube in a way entirely different from what he had proposed. Also, as he was at home when they made the discovery, he was afraid that he might not get all the credit. He immediately went into seclusion and worked around the clock to create an advanced version of the transistor that would upstage what they had discovered."

"When photos of the moment of the breakthrough were staged for the press, Shockley grabbed the seat that Brattain had been in when the discovery was made, creating the impression that he had made the discovery. At a press conference, Shockley also gave the false impression that Brattain was simply following his instructions. He tried in vain to convince patent attorneys that his should be the only name on the patent. Although the Nobel Prize for the transistor was awarded to all three men, Bardeen and Brattain were deeply troubled by Shockley's attempt to take all the credit."

"When Shockley started his own company, he tried to hire scientists from AT&T. Each one turned him down, so he hired scientists who didn't know him well. Within his company, Shockley controlled the work of the scientists so much, they could not pursue their own ideas. Scientists with leadership ability became frustrated. They found other opportunities and left to create Fairchild Semiconductors and Intel. Shockley's company failed."

"Many leaders have known how to find great opportunity and seize it. Many of them also could attract investors and deliver the benefits. But, like Shockley, some of them never developed others into innovators or high achievers or leaders of innovators and high achievers. Such leaders believe that only they can achieve at a high level and that they lose something when others succeed. They may fear that they will lose power, followers, control, or the chance to achieve again.

So the questions are:
- Why should we develop others?
- How should we develop others?

"Compare Shockley with Sam Walton. Sam Walton was an innovator and a high achiever who developed others for their benefit and for the benefit of his organization. Early in the development of Wal-Mart, he realized that one of the great pitfalls of expanding a business was in not developing strong leader-managers. He also knew how much retail management expertise it took to become a strong leader-manager. So Sam went after leaders. In his words, 'Without shame or embarrassment, I

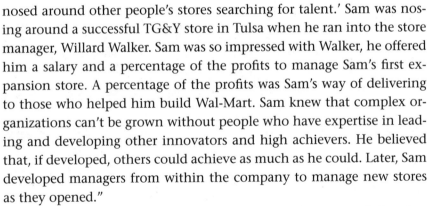

12. Develop other innovators and high achievers
- Why should we develop others?
- How should we develop others

nosed around other people's stores searching for talent.' Sam was nosing around a successful TG&Y store in Tulsa when he ran into the store manager, Willard Walker. Sam was so impressed with Walker, he offered him a salary and a percentage of the profits to manage Sam's first expansion store. A percentage of the profits was Sam's way of delivering to those who helped him build Wal-Mart. Sam knew that complex organizations can't be grown without people who have expertise in leading and developing other innovators and high achievers. He believed that, if developed, others could achieve as much as he could. Later, Sam developed managers from within the company to manage new stores as they opened."

"Developing others is an important leadership responsibility. Our next leader, Phil Jackson, is a master of both. He has helped some of basketball's best players to become leaders of high achievers."

The "Jordan Problem"

"By nineteen eighty-nine, Michael Jordan was the best basketball player and the leading scorer in the NBA. Because he could take control of a game at will, competitors feared him, and his teammates were in awe of him. But the Bulls' head coach, Doug Collins, and his staff regularly discussed what they called the 'Jordan Problem.'[111] Because Jordan was the Bulls' major scoring threat, other teams beat them by double-teaming him. Teammates keyed their play around him, reluctant to initiate plays independently."

"The Bulls attempted many solutions. In one staff meeting, assistant coach Phil Jackson said that Red Holzman believed the mark of a great player was not how much he scored but how much he lifted his teammate's performances. Collins told Jackson to tell that to Jordan. Reluctantly, Jackson approached Jordan in the weight-training room and told him Holzman's point of view. Jordan thanked him for the advice."

"The following season, Jordan agreed to become a point guard, direct the offense, and bring other players into the action. It seemed to work, at first. But, by the time the Bulls lost in the Eastern Conference finals, it was clear that, after running as point guard and directing the offense, Jordan didn't have the energy left for the last quarter drive."

"When Jackson became head coach of the Chicago Bulls, he searched for an opportunity to lift the whole team to championship level. He decided that he needed to replace its traditional power offense.[112]

"Jackson felt that a power offense was creative in the hands of a great player like Jordan, but it involved only two or three players in any given play. He needed an offense that involved all the players in a play. He decided to change to a triangle offense designed by assistant coach Tex Winters."

"Jackson had to persuade Jordan to try the triangle offense and to lead the team in a way that helped the other players to become high achievers and come together as a team. He had to replace the meaning Jordan would lose as the team star. He had to sell Jordan the idea that helping his teammates to be all they could be was the key to an NBA title."

"In his book, *Sacred Hoops*, Jackson recalls the conversation he had with Jordan, in which he asked Jordan to help him lead the switch to a new triangle offense and to share the spotlight with his teammates in order to help them grow into high achievers."

Jordan: Well, I think we're going to have trouble when the ball gets to certain people, because they can't pass and they can't make decisions with the ball.

Jackson: I understand that. But I think if you give the system a chance, they'll learn to be playmakers. The important thing is to let everybody touch the ball, so they won't feel like spectators. You can't beat a good defensive team with one man. It's got to be a team effort.

Jordan: Okay, you know me. I've always been a coachable player. Whatever you want to do, I'm behind you.

"From that time on, Jordan devoted himself to making the new system work, and Jackson devoted himself to persuading each player to surrender his 'me' for the 'we' of being part of a team with a great mission. Beginning in nineteen ninety-one, the Bulls jelled as a team and won three straight NBA titles."

"Today, Jackson has nine NBA titles—as many as anyone in NBA history. He elevates the players and the team above himself. Although some argue that his teams won just because they had great players, Shaquille O'Neal knows better. After Jackson left the Bulls, he moved to LA and led the LA Lakers, with O'Neal, to three straight NBA titles. O'Neal said he would have no title rings if it were not for Jackson. Shaquille O'Neal and Michael Jordan played a combined thirteen seasons and never won a championship without Phil Jackson as coach."

"Mike," Marcus said, "you helped many of the employees at Dardenn to develop and you take pride in their success. They will still look to you for leadership."

I shook my head. "I'm trying to keep Paul from getting fired, but the rest of them are afraid to do anything except what Ron and Larry want. Thanks for the compliment, though. I haven't been much help as a reviewer of your research. You have this well thought out. I feel more like a student. Did you ask me to come only because you wanted my opinions?"

"No, I hoped that I would interest you enough that you'd join me in teaching these actions to others around the world. However, I now know that you're in a critical position at Dardenn."

"I'm needed there right now," I said. "Maybe later. . . ." I stopped short of committing.

"Yes," he said, "after you get Dardenn back on track."

He was quiet for a moment. Then he said, "Let's make use of the time we have."

Future Innovators And High Achievers Are Made

He resumed walking. "For centuries, people debated why it was that some individuals became great," he said, "whether it was God-given ability, the right early environment, perseverance, courage, hard work, or luck. Alexander the Great and Napoleon Bonaparte, who were larger-than-life military leaders, often are cited as examples of great leaders who were born to lead. As I said before, Alexander was the son of a king and a princess, and Aristotle taught him. Napoleon's father was a lawyer, and Napoleon was educated at the prestigious Brienne and the Ecole Militaire."

"However, for every Alexander and Napoleon, history provides examples of people born to power and privilege who were low achievers and poor leaders. For example, Louis XVI was the grandson of a king, and his wife, Marie Antionette, was the daughter of an Emperor and Empress. Louis was weak and incapable and preferred to spend his time playing instead of leading. While the country was in financial crises, Marie flaunted her wealth. When hungry mobs marched on the palace, she refused to make any concessions and set the troops on them. At a time of great crises, both of them failed."

Marcus stopped, turned a few pages in the manuscript, handed it to me opened, and pointed to a drawing.

"The drawing shows that developing leaders of innovators and high achievers is at the top of the pyramid of leadership expertise," he said. I don't believe that innovators, high achievers or great leaders are born with all the skills to succeed. Even if they are, they still must be developed. Great leaders know that people and organizations must be taught to take powerful actions to reach their potential.

"By the time the Second World War occurred, Eisenhower and Churchill were already near the top of the achievement pyramid. Most

Innovator and High Achiever Development

great leaders, such as Fred Smith, Oprah Winfrey, Dwight Eisenhower, Sam Walton, Winston Churchill, and Abraham Lincoln, rose from the bottom to the top of the pyramid. They knew that leaders are made and that leadership could be taught. Much of the writing of the great leaders had a leadership theme."

Marcus slowed his walk as we reached an iron gate at the entrance to a fortress-like building. "This is Palazzo Medici-Riccardi, former home of the rich and powerful Lorenzo de Medici," he said. "Lorenzo brought Michelangelo to live here after he discovered Michelangelo's talent." He waved to a man inside who waved back and swung the gates open.

What Is Above Knows What Is Below

. . . There is an art of conducting oneself in the lower regions by the memory of what one saw higher up.

When one can no longer see, one can at least still know.

Rene Daumal[113]

Courtyard

We passed through the gate and walked to an interior courtyard that was open to a cloudless blue sky. The sounds of the street had disappeared. Marcus spoke reverently; his words echoed from ancient walls. "Mike, when I want to be inspired, I come here. I wish I could help you find the opportunity you need right now. I don't know the answer but I know that innovative leadership is the result of mastering both high-leverage and high-meaning expertise.

The Mystical Part Of Expertise

"With the actions for finding great opportunities, we maximize the chances that we'll find the great opportunities of our time. With the actions to mobilize support, we can find the highest meanings of others and motivate them to invest their time, ideas, and resources. With the actions to seize great opportunities, we can rapidly seize the opportunities and deliver the rewards."

He paused. "At the core of the actions for finding and seizing great opportunities is seeing David in the stone, and that's the mystical part of the expertise.

"This palace is where Lorenzo brought Michelangelo—a promising teenaged artist—and this is where Michelangelo first began to

169

think mystically. Many of the fine poets, writers, and philosophers that Lorenzo brought here were followers of the ancient Greek philosopher, Plato. Plato believed that people, buildings, and mountains are imperfect copies of ideal forms that exist in the ideal realm. He said that our souls come from the ideal realm and that we can remember these ideal forms if we search deeply for them. Young Michelangelo absorbed these ideas and combined them with his Christian beliefs. He came to believe that the ideal form was an idea held in the mind of God, and it was his creative task to see it and to free it from its marble bonds."

"That is why Michelangelo saw David staring at Goliath, the enemy, at the moment of decision, not at the moment of triumph—as other artists had. Before he began to carve, he saw where David was in the stone."

"As I said earlier, in addition to using the actions of the great innovators and achievers, we are looking at their seemingly mystical ability to see opportunities that others don't see. You need this mystical ability now more than ever."

Marcus's words seemed a bit unreal compared to the reality I was facing at Dardenn. I wanted to tell him that I had been pushed aside at Dardenn but I didn't. "I need a miracle," I said.

"I'll say it again; you'll find it," he assured me. "Search for it in high-leverage, high-meaning actions. Ask yourself, 'where do I have leverage with the Dardenn brothers?' Remember that Ron is an eager investor; where can you co-create with him? Where can you apply your small resources to move the whole company?"

During the walk back to the apartment, Marcus was silent. When we stood in front of the building, he reached out and shook my hand. "Mike, that's the end of our findings. I'll make changes to incorporate your insights. Thanks for taking the time to come here. I know this is a bad time for you to leave Dardenn, but if the time ever comes that you can, I hope you'll join me in teaching the actions of the great ones to others. As a past president of a successful corporation and as a former researcher, you would have great credibility."

"I'm honored that you want me to join you. That would be great. But you know I can't leave now."

"I understand," he said.

"Thanks for inviting me to review your work. I owe you," I replied.

Marcus handed me his card. "Call me if you need me—anytime." He smiled. "We'll meet again." He then turned around and walked to

the end of the block. From there, he waved to me and disappeared around the corner. Suddenly, I felt alone.

That evening, I followed the directions Marcus had given me to the village of Arcetri, where Galileo spent the last years of his life imprisoned in his home. The building was uninhabited and in disrepair. Looking through a gate into a courtyard overgrown with weeds, I imagined where the great thinker had sat and enjoyed the afternoon sun in the last years of his life.

I looked up at the balcony where Galileo probably had his telescope. I knew what he must have felt when he was banished. I thought about quitting. However, if I left, Ron would move all two thousand jobs to China or even sell the business. The employees welfare had no meaning to him.

Back at the apartment, I collapsed on the bed. I woke up four hours later, thinking about the turn my life had taken. Like Paul, when friends or neighbors lost their jobs, I never imagined that it would happen to me.

Knowing that I wouldn't be ready to go back to sleep for a while, I left the apartment to take a walk. It was a balmy night with no breeze and a perfectly clear sky—perfect for thinking about the mess at Dardenn. Marcus's words kept repeating in my mind: "You will find it. Search for it in the high-leverage, high-meaning actions." For the next few hours as I walked, I reviewed each action of the great ones, hoping for clues as to where an opportunity existed.

The sun woke me at six a.m. As I came to, I found the seed of an opportunity. The seed grew while I showered and dressed.

I left Florence early on Friday morning. On the long flight, I had plenty of time to think. Until Jesse died, my purpose at Dardenn was clear. Now, later in life, I was dealing with a very damaged stone. Seeing one's David in the stone is a lifelong quest, I thought.

I realized that I had to sell Ron the idea that, with Paul and me, he could take Dardenn to heights beyond what Jesse dreamed of.

The Meeting

I arrived in Ron's office early Saturday morning. He and Larry already were there.

Ron smiled, shook my hand, and patted me on the shoulder. "Mike, we all need to be on the same page."

I patiently listened to Larry argue that the vent should be removed and that firing Paul was necessary to put him in his place. Then I made a move.

I looked directly at Larry. "Larry, is your goal the same as Ron's, to take Dardenn beyond what Jesse had imagined?" He ignored what I said and demanded "We've got bigger fish to fry right now. Ron, are you going to tell Mike?"

Ron grimaced at Larry. Then he looked down at the floor while he spoke. "I need you to spend a lot of time in China. While you're there, Larry will cover your work here."

"Are you saying you're giving my job to Larry?"

"While you're in China," Ron said.

Larry snapped his head toward Ron. His face reddened. "You agreed to make me president permanently!"

Ron looked at his watch and said that he was late for a bank meeting.

"Not until we get this straight," Larry demanded.

Ron looked at Larry menacingly. "You have the job! Prove you can do it better than Mike. I'm the chairman of this company!"

"Only with my help," Larry shot back. "We had a deal."

Ron banged his fist on the conference table. "That's the last word." He got up and left the room.

Larry just sat there for a minute. Then he got up and stomped out.

I went back to my office and sat for a while, absorbing what had just happened. I tried to think of the good side. I was financially set for the rest of my life. I could sell my stock to one of the brothers and start my own company. I had my health and two great children. But I couldn't get over the fact that, after all the years of work, they wanted me out. And, I had a responsibility.

Digging through four days' mail, I noticed that twelve out of sixteen messages marked "urgent" or "important" were no longer important. Only one problem needed immediate attention. Nearly a hundred other messages, some more than a page long, were low leverage. I would have acted on every one of them. I promised myself to stop spending time and resources on low-leverage activities. One thing about losing your job: it sure puts a hundred e-mails in perspective.

The Proposal

Early Saturday afternoon, Larry pulled into my driveway. He looked strained. In rapid fire, he told me how much of their dad's money Ron had lost on two previous land-development schemes, that Ron was borrowing four million from the bank and was taking nine million from Dardenn's cash, and that he was going to build an office complex in Phoenix. He said that Ron wanted to prove he could make it in the land-development business. The bank requests suddenly made sense. "We have to stop him," Larry said.

"I'll talk to him," I said.

"No!" Larry said sharply. "Mike, he's going to get rid of you, and then he'll move some of our best people to Phoenix. If he isn't stopped, your stock will be worthless. I can help you."

"How?" I asked suspiciously.

"I have a backer who'll give me thirteen million to buy enough shares from you to give me control. You'll be set for life."

"What will happen to Ron?"

"I'll borrow the money to buy enough of his stock so he can do his land-development thing. It's a good deal for everybody."

"First, I'm going to try to talk Ron out of it."

Larry put his hand on my shoulder. "He'll just tell you what you want to hear," he said. "We can do this if we stick together."

After Larry left, I called Ron to tell him that I was on my way to his house to talk to him. He was in his front yard when I jumped from the car. "Ron, I've heard that you're planning to make an acquisition?"

He half-smiled. "I'm going to use our excess reserves to put us into the land-development business," he said. Like an excited kid, he explained the whole deal, including the nine million from cash reserves.

"It's too risky, and land development isn't our strength," I said.

"You have to take risks," Ron protested. "To make money, you have to spend money."

I had a momentary inclination to strike back at his patronizing cliché, but Marcus's voice was in my head, saying, "Can you negotiate with those who oppose you?"

"Ron, we invest three million each year in new-product startups, six million a year in capital improvements, and two million in personnel training and development."

He put his arm around me. "Super-safe investments," he said.

I turned toward him, to get his arm off my shoulder. "Ron, those investments fuel the almost one hundred ninety million in yearly sales, the nine-percent profit margin, and the nine million dollars in reserves. That's what it's going to take for you to take Dardenn beyond Jesse's growth goals"

The Showdown

Just then I saw Larry's car coming toward us. Larry pulled to the side of the road and screeched to a stop. He jumped out of the car and slammed the door. Coming toward us, he blurted out, "Did Mike tell you he came to me and offered to sell me his stock?"

Ron looked at me. "Is that right?"

"No," I said.

Ron stiffened. "Mike, I just want to hear if you're going to try to stop me from building the office complex in Phoenix.

"If I can, but. . . ."

Ron interrupted. "Well you can't," he said, pounding his finger into my lapel. He turned away from me. "Mike," his voice rose, "you've been plotting against me ever since I took over as chairman." He turned abruptly and walked toward his house.

Searching For Leverage

I drove to my office and closed the door. Marcus 's words came to mind. "Don't focus just on the problems. Look for the highest-leverage opportunity." The problem was that both brothers wanted to get rid of me so they could do their own things. And that wouldn't change. Larry wanted the company to own a racing team, and Ron wanted the company to be in land development. Where could I find a high-leverage opportunity in that?

There was a knock on the door. It was Mary. I waved her in and asked her what she was doing in the office on Saturday afternoon. "Mike, I'm worried about what Ron could do financially to this company. But I just figured a way that you could get control of the company by borrowing about nineteen million," she said. She smiled smugly. "Then I called my friend who's the vice president at the bank and asked if he thought that the bank would lend you the money to buy a majority of the stock. I told him it was urgent that I got an answer. He said he'd contact the bank president. He just called and said that with Dardenns' financial position and with you running the company, they would lend the money."

"Wow," I said, "that's the high-leverage opportunity I didn't see. Thanks, I'll see that you get a piece of the action if you want it."

"I want it," she said.

I called Ron, leaving an urgent message on his cell phone, saying that I had information critical to his project in Phoenix. Then I waited. Within an hour, Ron returned my call and asked to meet me at Jesse's house. I agreed, surprised by his choice of location.

Searching For Meaning

When I arrived, Ron's car was in the driveway and the front door was open. The living room looked like an abandoned mansion in an old movie, with white dust covers over the furniture.

Ron removed a white cover from a chair. I recognized it as Jesse's favorite chair. Looking directly into my eyes, he said, "I'm sure that Larry's already offered to buy your stock. If you sell your stock to Larry, he'll take over. Is that what you want?

I didn't answer. He hesitated and then said, "You do understand that, since Larry has over one-third of the stock, I have to put him in as president to get his voting rights?"

I stared at him.

"You know I wouldn't treat you that way unless I had to," he said.

I heard the front door open, and a trace of sunlight moved across the living room. In a moment, Larry was standing silhouetted in the light. What's going on?" he asked accusingly. "Are you two turning on me? No one answered him. "Damn you, you'll pay," he said. Then he was gone from the door.

We listened until his car's door slammed and the tires squealed. "Dad and I always protected him," Ron said. He looked passively at me. "Mike, it's your move."

The Spirit of Jesse Dardenn

I thought about the fifth action: find the highest meanings of others. "It seems to me that your passion and expertise is in land development," I said.

"True," Ron said with a sigh.

"I have an idea about how you can do your land development and still have Dardenn making money for you, without your involvement, for the rest of your life."

"I'm listening," he said.

I'll buy enough stock from you and Larry to own fifty-one percent of the stock."

"Mike, we're talking about nearly twenty million."

I nodded.

He stood and began to pace slowly.

"Ron, I promise you I will give my all to this company to make sure that your remaining stock investment grows in value."

"You could be a rich man if you sell your stock to me. Why are you doing this?" Ron asked.

"I have a promise to keep to Jesse," I said. "I owe him. He built a great thing, and I want to keep on building."

There was a long period of silence. Finally, Ron said "I believe you," He walked back to Jesse's chair and sat down. After what seemed like an eternity, he began to slowly nod his head. "Okay, it's a deal. I think the best way to do this is for you to buy enough from me to give you controlling interest. Once you're in control, Larry will see that his best interest is to sell me half of his stock and go on to something else."

I breathed a large sigh. Then I walked over to a portrait of Jesse. I said, "It feels like Jesse is in the room."

He smiled sadly, then turned his eyes away from me. I knew there was nothing more to say, so I headed toward the door.

"Mike, We'll get on it first thing Monday morning," he said softly, as I walked out.

On the way home, I stopped at a printer and had a poster-sized display of the twelve actions of the great ones made to hang in my office. "Thank you, Marcus," I said quietly, as I turned my car toward home.

Finding & Seizing Great Opportunities

Seize Great Opportunities
12. Develop other innovators and high achievers
11. Deliver rewards
10. Seize rapidly at high-leverage points
9. Use superior design and planning processes

Mobilize Support
8. Find common meaning with and negotiate with opposers
7. Sell the opportunity to those that are cautious
6. Co-create with those eager for opportunity
5. Find the highest meanings of others

Find Great Opportunities
4. Select only high-leverage opportunities
3. Learn to envision opportunities
2. Use powerful learning processes
1. Differentiate yourself for opportunity

END NOTES

Studying History's Greatest Finders And Seizers Of Opportunity

1. Jehl, Francis. (1937). *Menlo Park Reminiscences*. Dearborn, MI: Edison Institute. Republished 1990 by Dover Publications Inc., Mineola, NY.
2. Drucker, Peter F. (2001). *The Essential Drucker*. New York: Harper Business.
3. Yoshikawa, Eiji. (1981). *Musashi*. New York: Kodansha America.

The Twelve Actions Of The Great Innovators And Achievers

4. From a Michelangelo letter to his father.

Part I: Actions To Find Great Opportunities

5. Maxwell, John C. (1998). *The 21 Irrefutable Laws of Leadership*. Nashville, TN: Thomas Nelson.

Action 1. Differentiate Yourself For Opportunity

6. Wilson, Taylor Andrew. (2000). *The Mind Accelerator: Your Lexicon for Success*. New York: Volition Thought House.
7. Collins, Jim. (2001). *Good to Great*. New York: Harper Collins.
8. Collins, Jim. (2001). *Good to Great*. New York: Harper Collins.
9. Buckingham, Marcus, & Coffman, Curt. (1999). *First, Break All The Rules*. New York: Simon & Schuster. The authors analyzed 80,000 interviews with managers, conducted as part of a Gallup Survey.
10. Gatlin, Jonathan. (1999). *Bill Gates*. New York: Avon Books.

Action 2. Use Powerful Learning Processes

11. Whiting, Roger. (1992). *Leonardo*. New York: Knickerbocker Press.
12. Beckwith, Harry. (1997). *Selling the Invisible*. New York: Warner Books.
13. Rogers, Joel A. (1947). *World's Great Men of Color*. New York: Touchstone.
14. *Microsoft Encarta*. (1993-2000). Redmond, WA : Microsoft Corporation.
15. Goleman, Daniel, Kaufman, Paul, & Ray, Michael. (1992). *The Creative Spirit*. New York: Penguin Books.
16. Gardner, Howard. (1993). *Creating Minds*. New York: Basic Books.
17. Rabinow, Jacob. (1990). *Inventing for Fun and Profit*. San Francisco: San Francisco Press.
18. Klein, Burton. (1977). *Dynamic Economics*. Boston: Harvard University Press.
19. Jewkes, John, Sawers, David, & Stillerman, Richard. (1960). *The Sources of Invention*. London: Macmillan LTD.
20. Kay, John. (1998). *Microsoft® Encarta® 98 Encyclopedia*. Redmond, WA: Microsoft Corporation.
21. Whiting, Roger. (1998). *Leonardo: A Portrait of the Renaissance Man*. New York: Knickerbocker Press.

22. Randall, Willard Sterne. (1993). *Thomas Jefferson.* New York: Harper Collins.
23. Alexander, Christopher. (1979). *The Timeless Way of Building.* New York: Oxford University Press.
24. Morse, Gardiner. (2002, August). Conversation with Ed Catmull, "The Innovative Enterprise," *Harvard Business Review,* Special Issue, p.18.
25. Drucker, Peter F. (2001). *The Essential Drucker.* New York: Harper Business.
26. Drucker, Peter F. (2001). *The Essential Drucker.* New York: Harper Business.
27. Jenner, Bruce. (1996). *Finding the Champion Within.* New York: Simon & Schuster.
28. Gatlin, Jonathan. (1999). *Bill Gates.* New York: Avon Books.
29. Ornstein, Robert. (1991). *The Evolution of Consciousness.* New York: Touchstone/ Simon & Schuster.
30. Minsky, Marvin. (1985). *The Society of Mind.* New York: Simon & Schuster.
31. Tafel, Edgar. (1979). *Years With Frank Lloyd Wright: Apprentice to Genius.* New York: McGraw-Hill.
32. Schacter, Daniel L. (1996). *Searching for Memory: The Brain, the Mind, and the Past.* New York: Basic Books. Some brain scientists, including Schacter, use the words "elaborative encoding" instead of "deep processing."
33. The hippocampus in the mid-brain will decide to store information long-term if we repeat it, dwell on it, or if it arouses emotion. If all three are strong, the memory may last a lifetime.

Action 3. Learn To Envision Opportunities

34. Carroll, Lewis. (1893). *Through the Looking Glass.* New York: T. Y. Crowell & Co.
35. Gardner, Howard. (1993). *Creating Minds.* New York: Basic Books.
36. Stone, Irving. (1961). *The Agony and the Ecstasy.* New York: Signet.
37. "Poliomyelitis," In *Microsoft® Encarta® 98 Encyclopedia.* (1998). Redmond, WA: Microsoft Corporation.
38. Csikszentmahayli, Mihalyi. (1996). *Creativity.* New York: Harper Collins.
39. Csikszentmahayli, Mihalyi. (1996). *Creativity.* New York: Harper Collins.
40. Collins, Jim. (2001). *Good to Great.* New York: Harper Collins.
41. From an interview with Judy Anderson by James B. Swartz
42. Collins, Jim. (2001). *Good to Great.* New York: Harper Collins.
43. Levitt, Theodore. (2002, August). "The Innovative Enterprise." *Harvard Business Review.*
44. Nathan, John. (1995). *Sony, the Private Life.* New York: Houghton-Mifflin.
45. Drucker, Peter. (1964). *Managing for Results.* New York: Harper Collins.
46. Polya, G. (1957). *How to Solve It* (2nd ed.). Princeton, NJ: Princeton University Press/ New York: Doubleday.
47. Stone, Irving. (1961). *The Agony and the Ecstasy.* New York: Signet.
48. From interview with Cheryl Krueger by James B. Swartz.
49. Wallas, Graham. (1926). *The Art of Thought.* New York: Harcourt/Brace.
50. For some examples of games, go to www.seeingdavidinthestone.com or www. competiveaction.com
51. Stone, Irving. (1961). *The Agony and the Ecstasy.* New York: Signet.
52. A&E Television Networks. (1994). *Biography: Michelangelo: Artist and Man.* New York: Author.

Action 4. Select Only High-leverage Opportunity

53. Slater, Robert. (1999). *Jack Welch and the GE Way.* New York: McGraw Hill.
54. From interview with Cheryl Krueger by James B. Swartz.
55. Collins, Jim. (2001). *Good to Great.* New York: Harper Collins.

Part Ii: Actions To Mobilize Support

56. Jackson, Phil. (1995). *Sacred Hoops: Spiritual Lessons of a Hardwood Warrior.* New York: Hyperion.

Action 5. Find The Highest Meanings Of Others

57. Reston, James, Jr. (1994). *Galileo.* New York: HarperCollins.
58. Stone, Irving. (1961). *The Agony and the Ecstasy.* New York: Signet.
59. *Microsoft Encarta.* (2003). Redmond, WA : Microsoft Corporation.
60. *Microsoft Encarta.* (2006). Redmond, WA : Microsoft Corporation.
61. Adler, Bill. (1997) *The Uncommon Wisdom of Oprah Winfrey.* New York : Carol Publishing.
62. Stevens, Mark. (2001) *Extreme Management.* New York: Warner Business Books.
63. Drucker, Peter F. (2001). *The Essential Drucker.* New York: Harper Business.
64. Gibran, Kahlil. (1923). *The Prophet.* New York: Alfred E. Knopf.
65. MacArthur, Brian (Ed). (1996). *The Penquin Book of Historic Speeches.* New York: Penquin Books. The context in which the speech was given is on page 664 of Churchill, A Life, by Martin Gilbert (New York: Henry Holt and Company, 1991).
66. Landes, David S. (1998). *Why Are Some So Rich and Others So Poor?* New York: W.W. Norton.
67. Maslow, Abraham H. (1988). *Maslow on Management.* New York: John Wiley & Sons.
68. Frankl, Victor. (1984). *Man's Search for Meaning.* Boston: Beacon Press.
69. Frankl, Victor. (1984). *Man's Search for Meaning.* Boston: Beacon Press.

Action 6. Co-create With Those Eager For Opportunity

70. FedEx Annual Report for 2004, published by FedEx

Action 7. Sell Opportunity To Those That Are Cautious

71. Quinn, Daniel. (1992). *Ishmael.* New York: Bantam Books.
72. Rogers, Everett. (1995). *Diffusion of Innovations.* New York: The Free Press.
73. Ferguson, Marilyn. (1987). *The Aquarian Conspiracy.* Los Angeles: Jeremy .P.Tarcher/ New York: St. Martin's Press.
74. This would later become Isaac Newton's First Law of Motion.
75. From an interview with Louise Francesconi by James Swartz.

Action 8. Find Common Meaning With And Negotiate With Opposers

76. Maurer, Rick. (1996). *Beyond the Wall of Resistance.* Austin, TX: Bard Books. Maurer introduced us to the concept of embracing the resistance. He has concluded from his research that the ability to embrace the resistance is a key secret of those who are able to go beyond the "wall of resistance."
77. Fishman, Ted C. (2005). *China Inc.* New York; Scribner.
78. Maurer, Rick. (1996). *Beyond the Wall of Resistance.* Austin, TX: Bard Books.

Part III: Actions To Seize Great Opportunities

79. A&E Television Networks. (1994). *Biography: Michelangelo: Artist and Man.* New York: Author.

Action 9. Use Superior Design Processes

80. Bandrowski, James F. (1990). *Corporate Imagination Plus*. New York: Free Press.
81. Landrum, Gene N. (1993). *Profiles of Genius*. Buffalo, NY: Prometheus Books.
82. Covey, Steven. (1989). *The Seven Successful Habits of Highly Successful People*. New York: Fireside.
83. Lumet, Sidney. (1996). *Making Movies*. New York: Vintage Books.
84. Brooks, Frederick P., Jr. (1975). *The Mythical Man Month*. Reading, MA: Addison Wesley.
85. Curtis, Bill, Krasner, Herb, & Iscoe, Neil. (1988, November). A field study of the software design process for large systems. *Communications of ACM* (Association for Computing Machinery), 31, 11.
86. Walton, Sam, & Huey, John. (1992). *Made in America*. New York: Doubleday.
87. Kelley, Tom. (2001). *The Art of Innovation*. New York: Doubleday.
88. Drucker, Peter. (1964). *Managing for Results*. New York: Harper Collins.
89. Nickerson, Raymond S., Perkins, David N., & Smith, Edward E. (1985). *The Teaching of Thinking*. Hillsdale, NY: Lawrence Erlbaum Associates.
90. Nickerson, Raymond S., Perkins, David N., Smith, Edward E. (1985). *The Teaching of Thinking*. Hillsdale, NY: Lawrence Erlbaum Associates.

Action 10. Seize Rapidly At High-leverage Points

91. Senge, Peter. (1990). *The Fifth Discipline*. New York: Currency Doubleday. (Paperback edition, page 114.)
92. Hamm, Steve, & Greene, Jay. (2004, October 25). *The Man Who Could Have Been Bill Gates*. Business Week, pp. 106-108.
93. Carroll, Paul. (1993). *Big Blues: The Unmaking of IBM*. New York: Crown Publishing.
94. Senge, Peter. (1990). *The Fifth Discipline: The Art and Practice of the Learning Organization*. New York: Currency Doubleday.
95. Gilbert, Martin. (1991). *Churchill, A Life*. New York: Henry Holt and Company.
96. Stevens, Mark. (2001). *Extreme Management*. New York: Warner Business Books.
97. See the website www.seeingdavidinthestone.com
98. Dwight D. Eisenhower prepared for opportunity: He graduated from West Point and served successfully in many assignments in his early military career, acquiring expertise in military training, strategy, logistics, and battle tactics. He served as Chief of Staff under General Douglas MacArthur, who called him the best officer in the Army. Although he graduated in the middle of his class at West Point, when he attended the Army Command and General Staff School, he graduated at the top of his class of 300. Prior to Normandy, he commanded successful large-scale sea-to-land operations in North Africa and Sicily.
99. Ambrose, Stephen E. (1994). *D-Day*. New York: Touchstone, New York.
100. Eisenhower had great respect for Rommel because Rommel had inflicted heavy losses on Eisenhower's troops in the Kasserine Pass in North Africa.
101. Ambrose, Stephen E. (1994). *D-Day*. New York: Touchstone, New York.
102. Ambrose, Stephen E. (1994). *D-Day*. New York: Touchstone, New York.
103. The U.S. Marine Corps. (1994). *Warfighting: The U.S. Marine Corps Book of Strategy*. New York: Currency Doubleday.
104. Devlin, Gerard M. (1979). *Paratrooper*. New York: St. Martins Press.
105. Ambrose, Stephen E. (1990). *Eisenhower*. New York: Touchstone.

Action 11. Deliver Rewards

106. Chawla, Sarita, & Renesch, John. (1995). *Learning Organizations*. New York: Productivity Press.

107. Levering, Robert, Moskowitz, Milton, & and Katz, Michael. (1987). *The 100 Best Companies to Work for in America*. New York: New American Library.
108. Ralph Waldo Emerson may be the first to have said this.
109. Collins, Jim. (2001). *Good to Great*. New York: Harper Collins.

Action 13. Develop High Achievers

110. Tichy, Noel M. (2002). *The Leadership Engine*. New York: Harper Business
111. Jackson, Phil. (1995). *Sacred Hoops*. New York: Hyperion.
112. Jackson, Phil. (1995). *Sacred Hoops*. New York: Hyperion.
113. Daumal, Renè. (2004). *Mount Analogue*. Overlook TP

Index

PHOTO CREDITS

pg. 4 (Voting Machine) from *Electric World.* Sept. 26, 1891 p.241.

pg. 5 (Santa Croce) James B. Swartz.

pg. 9 (David by Donatello) James B. Swartz

pg. 13 (Campanille) James B. Swartz

pg. 15 (Young Einstein) young Einstein from Frontispiece of Slosson, Edwin Emery. *Easy Lessons in Einstein.* New York: Harcourt, Brace and Howe. 1920 TC.

pg. 23 (Frederick Douglas) Library of Congress.

pg. 39 (Fallingwater) Kathleen M. Swartz

pg. 45 (Marie Curie) in *Eminent chemists of our time* by Benjamin Harrow. New York: D. Van Nostrand Company 1920. credit.

pg. 49 (Leonardo da Vinci) Mueller Walde, Dr. Paul. Munchen: 1889. frontispiece.

pg. 52 (Judy Anderson) From Judy

pg. 59 (The Slaves) James B. Swartz.

pg. 60 (David, by Michelangelo) James B. Swartz.

pg. 60 (Head of David) Jon Sall.

pg. 64 (bronze sculpture) James B. Swartz.

pg. 66 (Cheryl Krueger) From Cheryl

pg. 70 (Ponte Vecchio Bridge) James B. Swartz

pg. 80 (Galileo Galilei?) Kathleen M. Swartz.

pg. 83 (mountain scene?) James B.Swartz

pg. 86 (President Abraham Lincoln) from *Harper's Weekly* April 27, 1861

pg. 89 (John Mariotti) from John

pg. 90 (Winston Churchill) in *The Capitol, a Pictorial History of the Capitol.* Gov. Publication. House Document No. 96-374. p. 150

pg. 103 Norm Bodek from Norm

pg. 105 (Louis Pasteur) in Williams-Ellis, Annabel. *Men who Found Out.* New York: Coward McCann. 1930 p. 167 bit reapplied

pg. 134 (café) James B. Swartz

pg. 147 (Thomas Edison) from Darrow, Floyd. Masters of Science and Invention. N.Y. Harcourt Brace and Co. 1923. p. 320

pg. 151 (Dwight D. Eisenhower) in Nasa on line.

pg. 171 (village of Arcetri) James B. Swartz.

Aperio Group

- Concentrated portfolios that a client desires to diversify into a portfolio more representative of the broader market, such as the S&P 500, the Russell 3000, or any number of other market baskets. Aperio quantifies the tax cost of diversification and helps clients evaluate the trade-off between tax costs and the risk reduction that comes from diversification.

- Low-basis stock that a client may not want to sell due to adverse tax consequences. The strategy results in future heirs receiving a stepped-up basis, thereby permanently reducing taxes paid.

Incorporate Customized Social Screens

Many investors prefer to reflect their social values in the types of investments they make. With other co-mingled socially conscious portfolios, investors are forced to accept someone else's social screens rather than being able to define their own. Aperio can customize your portfolio to combine your own personal social values while allowing you to benefit from all the advantages of indexing.

For more information

Contact Guy Lampard at
Phone: (415) 339-4303
Fax: (415) 339-4301
Email: info@aperiogroup.com
Website: www.aperiogroup.com

Portfolio Construction

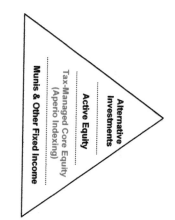

Alternative Investments

Active Equity

Tax-Managed Core Equity
(Aperio Indexing)

Munis & Other Fixed Income

Aperio Group LLC
Customized Portfolios for Taxable Investors

COMPANY PROFILE

Aperio Group delivers customized asset management services for taxable investors. Aperio designs and manages customized portfolios that deliver the pre-tax performance of indexing with active tax management and active risk reduction. The result is superior *after-tax* returns and reduced risk.

At Aperio we create customized portfolios of individual securities to:

- Maximize after-tax returns
- Reduce the risk of concentrated positions
- Incorporate customized social screens

Maximize After-Tax Returns

Aperio helps clients develop and implement investment strategies to maximize *after-tax* returns. We utilize cutting-edge multi-factor risk models and sophisticated tax-loss harvesting programs to help us maximize *after-tax* returns while minimizing tracking differences versus the target index. This process allows us to take advantage of the capital loss rules by selling securities in the portfolio that have declined and immediately replacing them with similar securities. The resulting real tax losses can then be used to shelter gains even from outside the portfolio, including capital gains realized by other active managers or gains realized from diversifying concentrated low-basis portfolios.

AT A GLANCE

Firm
Aperio Group LLC

Location
Three Harbor Drive
Suite 315
Sausalito, CA 94965

Aperio Portable Tax Alpha Strategies
Aperio offers customized tax-managed portfolios designed to track the following equity market indices:

- U.S. Total Market: Russell 3000 Index
- U.S. Large Companies: Russell 1000 Index or S&P 500 Index
- U.S. Small Companies: Russell 2000 Index
- U.S. Socially Responsible (SRI) Companies: Domini 400 Social Index
- Foreign: MSCI EAFE (ADR and ordinary shares); MSCI ACWI ex. U.S.

APERIO'S PORTFOLIO MANAGEMENT PROCESS

Aperio integrates BARRA's multiple factor model (MFM) and a sophisticated tax lot accounting system to construct and rebalance our tax managed, customized and index portfolios. Aperio's MFM describes over 9,000 stocks according to 13 risk factors (including volatility, momentum, market size, earnings yield, P/B ratio, dividend yield, trading activity, and leverage), 13 industry sectors and 54 industries. Our tax lot accounting system tracks each equity position by tax basis and date of purchase.

Our optimization program allows us to construct and rebalance our client portfolios while taking into consideration multiple constraints and allowing for multiple tax rates for long and short-term capital gains.

Objective

Deliver pre-tax returns similar to target market or custom index and maximize *after-tax* returns.

Parameters

Tracking error versus tax-efficiency, portfolio size, transaction costs (including bid-offer spreads) and level of portfolio customization.

ANSWERS TO COMMONLY ASKED QUESTIONS ABOUT APERIO'S SERVICES

With indexing, don't I just settle for average performance?

Indexing provides consistently above-average returns, as shown by numerous research studies on equity mutual funds. Over the long-term the Russell 3000 Index has beaten about 65-80% of active equity managers' pre-tax returns, depending on the time period. When comparing *after-tax* returns, active managers fare much worse due to their high fees and tax-inefficiency.

Why should investors care about taxes when evaluating performance?

Money managers rarely calculate after-tax returns and most portfolio management systems are not equipped to measure the impact of taxes. Yet, while high pre-tax returns help portfolio managers win performance rankings, taxable investors get to keep only a portion of that return. Studies have shown that taxable investors typically surrender 2-3% of portfolio return to federal taxes. The combination of tax drag and poor performance (active managers typically under-perform their pre-tax index benchmarks by more than 1.5%) makes active management a poor alternative for maximizing after-tax returns.

How can Aperio's clients use the benefit of a realized loss?

Realized losses can be used by investors to offset the same